T0275291

go *in* — The Art of Hearing Confessions
PEACE

JULIA GATTA *and* **MARTIN L. SMITH**

Morehouse Publishing
NEW YORK · HARRISBURG · DENVER

Morehouse Publishing, 4775 Linglestown Road, Harrisburg, PA 17112
Morehouse Publishing, 445 Fifth Avenue, New York, NY 10016
Morehouse Publishing is an imprint of Church Publishing Incorporated.

www.churchpublishing.org

Cover design by Laurie Klein Westhafer
Typeset by Denise Hoff

Library of Congress Cataloging-in-Publication Data

Gatta, Julia, 1948–

Go in peace : the art of hearing confessions / Julia Gatta, Martin L. Smith.

p. cm.

ISBN 978-0-8192-2088-2 (pbk.) -- ISBN 978-0-8192-2089-9 (ebook)
1. Confession. 2. Absolution. 3. Penance. 4. Pastoral theology --
Anglican Communion. 5. Anglican Communion--Doctrines. I. Smith,
Martin Lee. II. Title.

BV845.G38 2012

265'.62 -dc23

2012023086

We dedicate this book to two faithful priests
Martin to Robert K. Myers
Julia to William S. Stafford

with gratitude

CONTENTS

FOREWORD

One of the unintended consequences of providing the Sunday liturgy in an easy-to-use leaflet or booklet form is that congregations become increasingly unfamiliar with the contents of the Book of Common Prayer. Taken as a whole, the prayer book is the ritual celebration of the seasons of our lives from birth to death in the light of the gospel and the daily, weekly, and annual cycles that shape and determine our existence.

For many Episcopalians, a seemingly innocent perusal of its pages has been a pathway to faith. Among the more surprising discoveries for some has been the form for the Reconciliation of a Penitent. From time to time someone has approached me and asked, "What is this? I didn't know that the Episcopal Church had confession." This initial sense of surprise has sometimes been an enticement of the Spirit to explore further, and led those who raised the initial question to seek the healing grace of the sacramental rite for themselves.

The classical Anglican position regarding "making one's confession" in the presence of a priest is, "All may, some should, none must." For many, the forms of corporate confession of sin—such as the General Confession—that occur in the public rites of the church are sufficient. For others, and I include myself, it is all too easy, as Julia Gatta and Martin Smith observe, to murmur the familiar penitential phrases along with the rest of the congregation without any real sense of personal sinfulness or, for that matter, of God's healing and reconciling mercy and forgiveness proffered through the words of the absolution.

For many who avail themselves of the rite of reconciliation, the discipline of self-examination under the guidance of the Holy Spirit in preparation for making their confession in the presence of a priest can be an exercise in self-knowledge. We find ourselves drawn beyond particular events and acts into an ever-deepening understanding of the motivations of which our sins are an outward expression. This becomes particularly true when making our confession becomes a regular part of our spiritual practice.

As one who has since my teenage years regularly availed himself of this sacramental rite, and as a priest and bishop been called to "hear confessions" numerous times in the course of a wide-ranging pastoral ministry, I welcome this wise and careful exposition of the art of presiding at this sacramental encounter with God's mercy and profligate compassion. Julia Gatta and Martin Smith are eminently qualified, both as experienced priests and penitents, to offer guidance to members of the clergy who may be unfamiliar with or unprepared to offer this ministry of healing and reconciliation. A point our authors make, and one that cannot be stressed enough, is that those who preside at this rite need also to present themselves as penitents and surrender to the same sacramental encounter that they, in the name of the Church, mediate to others.

Go in Peace, therefore, is not simply about imparting a pastoral competency, but an invitation to those who are ordained as ministers of word and sacrament to avail themselves of this sacramental encounter with the risen Christ for their own soul's health. For it is in this way that those who act as confessors will bring to it their own experience of poverty before the Lord, and also have an intimate knowledge of how it "feels" to be a penitent. The only sure way in which a confessor can appreciate the delicacy and sensitivity required on his or her part in receiving the confession of another is by having been there. Before I was ordained, there were times when I had to coach an inexperienced priest in the midst of making my confession. And there have also been times when, instead of experiencing God's forgiveness, I have felt accused and judged by the aggressive line of query or comment on the part of a confessor unmindful of the vulnerability one feels as a penitent.

Another important point Gatta and Smith make is that the rite of reconciliation, rather than being penitential in tone, is an occasion of joyful release and return to the One whose forgiveness is without bounds: "As far as the east is from the west, so far has he removed our sins from us" (Psalm 103:12). While restitution or amends may be in order, a "penance" is better though of as an act of thanksgiving for the fact that "the Lord has put away all your sins."

The second half of *Go in Peace* contains a series of sample confessions involving men and women in different states and places in their lives. Here the authors' suggestions for advice and counsel that follow each confession are filled with wisdom. They display a sensitivity to the dynamics of receiving and responding to the insights and gifts each penitent may bring that can greatly benefit both new and experienced confessors.

Julia Gatta and Martin Smith have provided us with an invaluable resource, as well as the challenge to make this gift of grace more available as a normative ministry of the church. It is a gift that those who receive the confessions of others are invited to avail themselves of as well.

Frank T. Griswold
XXV Presiding Bishop
31 July 2012 (Ignatius of Loyola)

PART ONE

"Repent, and believe in the good news" (Mark 1:15)

CHAPTER ONE

Why Confession?

It is strange that sacramental confession to a priest is considered, even by clergy, to be something of a specialized or marginal ministry. The opening message of the gospels, announced by John the Baptist, reiterated by Jesus, and finally proclaimed by the apostles, is "Repent, and believe in the good news" (Mark 1:15). The grace to change one's mind and heart and then accept God's forgiveness lies at the very core of salvation. It represents the renewal of creation that is inaugurated by the resurrection of Jesus. Thus for those who have been baptized and who sin, as all adult Christians do, the practice of confession and absolution can be a significant sacramental encounter with the Christ who pardons, heals, and embraces us in love. It can signal a dramatic turning point or serve as one of many small conversions along the Christian journey.

Curiously, those outside the church or who work alongside it sometimes appreciate the role of confession more than those within it. So, for example, participants in Twelve Step programs know how crucial steps four through ten are to recovery: making a "searching and fearless moral inventory," confessing one's wrongs to God and another person, and seeking restitution and forgiveness whenever possible. Similarly, therapists know that a breakthrough to healing will only take place once sufficient trust has been established for clients to face the painful facts of the past, often hidden for years even from themselves, and finally disclose them.

Literature abounds with examples of confession. Consider Arthur Dimmesdale, perhaps the most self-tortured pastor in fiction. When Hawthorne's *The Scarlet Letter* begins, his adultery with Hester Prynne has already been committed, but Dimmesdale's anguish steadily grows with the silence of his unconfessed sin. Only at the very end, on the scaffold, does he make a clean breast of it and is set free. Even the children in C. S. Lewis' Narnia books have confidential interviews with Aslan after they have gone astray. At Peter's very first meeting with Aslan in *The Lion, the Witch and the Wardrobe*, when Mr. Beaver has revealed Edmond's betrayal to the great lion, something prompts Peter to confess:

> "That was partly my fault, Aslan. I was angry with
> him and I think that helped him to go wrong."
>
> And Aslan said nothing either to excuse Peter or
> to blame him but merely stood looking at him with
> his great unchanging eyes.

Later, when Edmond comes to his senses, he does not simply slip back into the fellowship he had broken, no questions asked. First there must be a crucial meeting with Aslan, but not even the reader is privy to that confession: "There is no need to tell you (and no one ever heard) what Aslan was saying, but it was a conversation that Edmond never forgot."[1]

Similarly, a recently composed play entitled *Mercy Me* dramatizes in its surprise ending how the exercise of confession engenders spiritual

---

1   C.S Lewis, *The Lion, the Witch and the Wardrobe* (New York: Scholastic, 1950), 128, 139.

and psychic recovery. Here playwright David Roby portrays a rural North Carolina family riddled with illness and dark secrets. They live on the edge of what was once the ancestral tobacco plantation, in a renovated distillery where the filth and squalor of their living quarters is more than matched by the bleakness of each inhabitant's life. Towards the end of the play, a self-styled "death coach," using the techniques of a personal trainer, shows up to lead the family in a ritualized communal confession. Very slowly, each character addresses God or the others present. Around they go, round robin, each reluctantly giving voice to some deep sorrow or longing. A communal mantra takes shape as they drone out their confessions and prayers. The tempo quickens as they repeat the exercise, eventually reaching a feverish pitch, and then slows as the characters befriend their painful disclosures, listen to each other, and silently release one another. At last, a quiet peace settles on this volatile family group.

Recognizing Sin

"The pious fellowship permits no one to be a sinner," observes Dietrich Bonhoeffer with stinging sarcasm in *Life Together*. In his powerful chapter on confession, this theologian strips away the façade, cultivated in some congregations, of being somehow above sin. Denial of sin, however, is not unique to the church. *Mercy Me* portrays a household, not unlike the human family itself, that has strong taboos in place to keep up the appearance of blamelessness. The deceptions of pride can be entrenched even when every other prop of social standing has collapsed. Only when pressed to an arduous exercise in truth-telling—one that needed to be doggedly repeated—could members of this family begin to find their true selves, and then let themselves be changed. Reconciliation is both sheer gift and personally costly. Yet finally it is the only way out.

In *Life Together* Bonhoeffer charged that too many churches had become enclaves of respectability, a situation that has not improved and may have possibly worsened since he first wrote about the need to recover the practice of personal confession in the church. *Life Together* was itself the fruit of Bonhoeffer's reflections on the disciplines and graces of Christian life in community, forged during the two years he served as director of a small, clandestine Lutheran seminary at Finkenwalde in northern Germany. He had been called to that ministry in 1935 by the Confessing Church—so named because it "confessed the faith" in the face of the German Reich church controlled by Nazi ideology. While Bonhoeffer never alludes in this book to the threatening conditions under which the seminary struggled, which was eventually closed by the Nazis, this political backdrop lends power and poignancy to his plea to "confess your sins to one another" as the Apostle James directs (James 5:16). Even when surrounded by the horrifying crimes of the Nazi regime, Bonheoffer did not lose sight of the reality of personal sinfulness either in himself or in the most devout, courageous, and committed members of the church. To see sin in others, while glossing over sin in oneself, is to forfeit the grace of the gospel. All stand in need of a savior.

A culture of stalwart respectability builds an impenetrable wall against truth-telling. In most mainline churches people drop out, at least for a while, when life gets messy. An impending divorce, an adulterous affair, chronic depression, a job layoff, a child in trouble with the law: all these commonplace occurrences drive people from the church just when they most need the grace of the sacraments and the support of the community. Pastors find themselves tracking down the lost sheep. And why do they disappear? Because the missing members are ashamed or confused, fearful that their neighbors might "judge" them or think ill of their failures as spouses, parents, and solid citizens. Someone might even think them guilty of sin. When Bonhoeffer asserts, "The pious fellowship permits no one to be a sinner," he goes on to observe that as a consequence of this suffocating pretension "everybody must conceal his sin from himself and from the fellowship. We dare not be sinners. Many Christians are unthinkably horrified when a real sinner is suddenly discovered among the righteous. So we remain alone with our sin, living in lies and hypocrisy."[2] Today "the pious fellowship" is most plainly evident in those places where sin itself is never mentioned. There exist numerous communities, some of them nominally Christian, that are committed to being relentlessly upbeat and cheerful no matter what. Sin is never mentioned, unpleasant topics like death are avoided, and preaching on the cross is proscribed. Yet even in mainstream liberal and conservative congregations, more subtle forms of "the pious fellowship" are also at work.

At first this can seem surprising; we might expect evangelical Christians to be at home with the language of sin and grace. After all, evangelicals are predisposed to grant that since "grace saved a wretch like me," it might also save a wretch like you. Sin, then, does not shock such people, but their readiness to acknowledge sinfulness pertains, for the most part, to our condition before conversion to Christ. An unanticipated dilemma can arise as the continued strength of sin *after* conversion is, perhaps reluctantly, detected. In some quarters, true conversion is presumed to be completed in one stroke. Consequently, there is little, if any, guidance on hand for the daily struggle with ingrained patterns of sin because real Christians have been "saved" from it. When the prevailing religious culture does not recognize that conversion is actually a lifelong process with many failures and falls, then one might indeed resort to "living in lies and hypocrisy" when the facts tell another tale entirely. With no inherited wisdom for coming to grips with our deeply rooted habits of sin, therefore, either despair or self-righteousness is apt to set in—despair for the more self-aware and self-righteousness for those who cannot, or will not, face themselves. The undertow of "the pious fellowship" sets everyone up for a conspiracy of silence about the ongoing presence of sin in our personal and communal life.

Self-righteous smugness infects liberal churches by another route. Here the focus shifts to social sin as the real arena of wrongdoing. These

---

2 Dietrich Bonhoeffer, *Life Together*, trans. John W. Doberstein (New York: Harper and Row, 1954), 110.

progressive congregations rightly emphasize the ways in which injustice permeates the social fabric through such evils as economic inequities, racial prejudice, gender bias, excessive national pride, and the waste and misuse of the earth. Biblically grounded preachers in these churches are able, sometimes eloquently, to interpret these ills in the light of the Old Testament, especially the prophets, as well as the teachings of Jesus. But other liberal preachers rehearse a wholly predictable diatribe, week after week, which can fool the congregation into thinking too highly of its righteous politics. Conservative churches are also concerned about the sins that afflict and weaken society as a whole, but more frequently the offenses they address are personal sins writ large, such as the sexual scandals or financial dishonesty of public figures, infidelity, divorce, abortion, drug addiction, and teenage pregnancies. In fact so much attention is directed towards sexual lapses that one wonders whether anything else really counts as sin. This problem is compounded when such churches claim to occupy the higher moral ground on issues under serious and thoughtful debate elsewhere in the church.

In both liberal and conservative churches, therefore, the prevailing culture "permits no one to be a sinner" because the sin under discussion always seems to be the sort of infuriating fault of which *other people* are guilty. Sin is what those other people commit—the kind of people who probably vote differently from the way I do. Because the culture wars have polarized Christians along with everyone else, the valuable social critique offered by some more conservative churches often gets discounted by those outside their circle, while the social sins brought to light by liberal churches are dismissed by conservatives as evidence of their captivity to secular humanism. When churches are talking only to themselves, busily shoring up their own passionately held convictions, no fresh word of truth can penetrate the wall of self-righteous indignation. The truly prophetic utterance which, as in ancient Israel, addresses both personal and social sin cannot be heard. So the sins that are never named in one's particular religious enclave grow in power. Having been banned from discussion, they remain hidden, exercising covert force.

A serious naiveté about sin permeates all sectors of the church for many reasons, including the loss of a vocabulary to identify specific sins. The church used to be fluent in this language, but fluency has been replaced by the deadening moralism of both right and left or by pop psychology masquerading as spirituality. Yet an awareness of the ascetical tradition of the church is an essential foundation for "the defense against the dark arts," to borrow an apt phrase from J. K. Rowling. It gives us basic tools to discern what is going on within and around us. Learning this tradition begins with the regular, probing, and meditative study of Scripture.[3] It also includes selective reading of the spiritual classics and some of their contemporary interpreters. For instance, in *Acedia & Me*, Kathleen Norris dramatizes for a general audience the value of comprehending the scope of this often misunderstood and overlooked deadly sin. By exploring the desert tradition and then combining it with personal narrative, Norris helps the reader move beyond the caricature of acedia (or sloth) as mere laziness to perceive its wide variations, including apathy, melancholy, and restlessness.[4] And we, like Norris, can also learn something about the subtleties of temptation and the paradoxes of grace by reflecting on our own experience of them against the backdrop of ascetical theology. When we engage in this work with the help of a seasoned spiritual director, we usually glean the greatest wisdom from both our encounters with grace and our inevitable lapses.

The clergy play a key role in the appropriation and articulation of this tradition. After decades of vocational drift in which clergy saw themselves as amateur psychological counselors, small- or large-scale managers, community organizers, or charismatic leaders, the demanding yet grace-filled work of simply being a pastor—that is, a shepherd of souls—is again coming to the fore. It is not that parish priests can or should escape their involvement with a large number of

---

3 See, for example, Martin L. Smith, *The Word is Very Near You: A Guide to Praying with Scripture* (Cambridge, MA: Cowley, 1989, 2006).
4 Kathleen Norris, *Acedia & Me: A Marriage, Monks, and A Writer's Life* (New York: Riverhead Books, 2008).

institutional responsibilities, including some fairly humdrum chores. It is rather a question of what they consider the center of this ministry to be, and what the ministry is for. In this more authentically pastoral perspective, institutional oversight and administration serve the cure of souls by helping to shape an environment in which growth in Christ can take place. As Eugene Peterson observes,

> Until about a century ago, what pastors did between Sundays was of a piece with what they did on Sundays. The context changed: instead of an assembled congregation, the pastor was with one other person or small gatherings of persons, or alone in study and prayer. The manner changed: instead of proclamation, there was conversation. But the work was the same: discovering the meaning of Scripture, developing a life of prayer, guiding growth into maturity. This is the pastoral work that is historically termed the cure of souls. The primary sense of *cura* in Latin is "care," with undertones of "cure." The soul is the essence of the human personality. The cure of souls, then, is the Scripture-directed, prayer-shaped care that is devoted to persons singly or in groups, in settings sacred or profane. It is the determination to work at the center, to concentrate on the essential . . . I am not contemptuous of running a church, nor do I dismiss its importance. . . . It is reducing pastoral work to institutional duties that I object to, not the duties themselves. [5]

As clergy recover their vocation as pastors charged with the cure of souls, they can begin to dispel the vacuous atmosphere of "the pious fellowship" as both sin and grace again become normal topics for pastoral conversation and preaching. Thundering against sin from the pulpit is

---

5 Eugene H. Peterson, *The Contemplative Pastor: Returning to the Art of Spiritual Direction* (Grand Rapids, MI: Eerdmans, 1989), 57, 59.

not the point. On the contrary, Christian preaching entails proclamation of the good news of Christ as it is embedded in the scriptural text and in life. But bland generalized assurances of divine love are not good news, and the effect of this sort of preaching is numbing over time. The deliverance proclaimed in the gospel is deliverance from *something*—and that something is summarized, in Scripture and in our liturgical texts, as the twin evils of sin and death. The lectionary provides vibrant examples of how grace overturns these evils as they appear, in a wide variety of forms and disguises, in particular situations and narratives. And we, like the cast of characters we encounter in the Bible, typically experience both sin and grace in richly textured, highly specific circumstances.

Baptism, Sin, and Forgiveness

No teaching about sin and salvation can stay purely theoretical for long. People have always wanted to see how it translates into daily living. For example, in the Acts of the Apostles, Luke presents the first proclamation of Jesus' death (a fact of common, public observation) and his resurrection (a matter of apostolic eyewitness) immediately after the coming of the Spirit on the Day of Pentecost. The Jerusalem crowd who hear Peter and the apostles are "cut to the heart" as they recognize both their sinful collusion in the death of Jesus and the wondrous grace of his resurrection from the dead. But they do not stay there for long, because the question that immediately arises after the gospel is preached, and people find themselves convicted of sin, is practical: "What should we do?" And over the centuries, the response of the church has been the same as that of Peter and the apostles: "Repent, and be baptized every one of you in the name of Jesus Christ so that your sins may be forgiven; and you will receive the gift of the Holy Spirit" (Acts 2:37–38). Baptism is the way this forgiveness gets inside us, and it forms the sacramental grounding for Christian life—a life animated and shaped by the Holy Spirit.

When a robust theology of baptism is preached and taught, it becomes the interpretive key to all our human experiences. Romans 6 is the foundational key text here, where Paul teaches that through baptism we have been united with Christ both "in a death like his" and "in a resurrection like his." Thus the union with Christ forged in baptism constitutes the basis of Christian spirituality and practice: all Christian life is, quite simply, life in Christ. The liturgical reforms that have restored baptism to its definitive place in the church have helped shape a more authentic baptismal identity among Christians, as both adults and children witness baptisms taking place within the Sunday eucharistic assembly at regular intervals. Opportunities to renew one's baptismal promises, especially for those baptized as infants or young children, at Confirmation, the Great Vigil of Easter, or whenever baptism is administered, lends gravity to the commitment and can deepen our awareness of what it means to share in the paschal mystery of Christ's death and resurrection.

The extraordinary grace of baptism evokes a heartfelt human response. In the same crucial passage in which Paul speaks of it as union with Christ in his death and resurrection, the apostle teases out the practical implications of what it means to share in the death of Christ. Prior to our own bodily death, it binds us to a daily spiritual death to sin: "So you also must consider yourselves dead to sin and alive to God in Christ Jesus" (Romans 6:11). In other words, there is an ascetical edge to baptism that should never be downplayed or underestimated. We are anointed in baptism with nothing less than the sign of the cross. This is no mere rite of warm, friendly inclusion. Both the demands and the grace of baptism mold Christian life at every turn. Dying to sin is hard, requiring self-knowledge, vigilance, labor, and many humiliating defeats. Still, the whole process is grounded in hope: all this toil is but one dimension of what it means to live in Christ, sharing at all times in his death and resurrection.

It should come as no surprise that the question, "What should we do?" also arises as Christians recognize their persistent entanglements with sin after baptism. For most people, baptized as infants, this is their sole experience of personal sin. The church's pastoral response to post-baptismal sin, however, has taken a variety of forms and approaches over the years. We can see some of this diversity within the New Testament itself. At one end of the spectrum, the Epistle to the Hebrews and the First Epistle of John reflect the most rigorous view. For these writers, at least one sin—the sin of apostasy—was actually considered beyond forgiveness (Hebrews 6:4–6; 1 John 5:16–17). As a repudiation of Christ by one who had received his grace, apostasy seems to constitute a permanent cancellation of the benefits of baptism, including the forgiveness of sin. Although 1 John urges Christians humbly to confess their persistence in sin in order to obtain divine mercy (2:1–2), the letter also states that there exists an exceptional case: a sin which inevitably leads to spiritual death. This is "mortal" sin, and no recovery from it can be expected. In this instance, prayer itself is rendered useless.

By contrast, when Paul exercises pastoral discipline in the churches under his authority, his overarching aim is to restore the offending party. Even in the extreme case of handing a notorious sinner "over to Satan for the destruction of the flesh," the ultimate purpose of excommunication is to ensure that "his spirit may be saved in the day of the Lord" (1 Corinthians 5:5). A still gentler approach may be found in the Epistle of James, which links healing with confession (James 5:13–16). When the letter urges the presbyters of the church to anoint the sick and pray over them, it then goes on to state that "anyone who has committed sins will be forgiven." In this context, the advice to confess sins "to one another" might be construed as a formal confession to the presbyters; more likely, however, it is recommending a kind of mutual confession of faults among Christians that also appears in other early Christian texts.[6]

The handing over of the "keys of the kingdom of heaven" with their power to "bind and loose" in Matthew 16:19 (to Peter) and 18:18 (to

---

6 Jeffery John, "'Authority Given to Men': The Doctrinal Basis of Ministerial Absolution in the New Testament," *Confession and Absolution*, ed. Martin Dudley and Geoffrey Rowell (Collegeville, MN: Liturgical Press, 1990), 15–39.

the apostles) would play a definitive role in the church's evolving understanding of its disciplinary prerogatives. In rabbinic circles, the expression to "bind and loose" referred to authoritative interpretations of the Law, and meant either to forbid or allow something. A related usage connected this faculty to imposing or lifting a ban of excommunication from the synagogue. The presence of this terminology in Matthew's gospel is significant. It indicates that this sort of rabbinic understanding informed the evangelist's community, that matters of forgiveness and church discipline were being handled along these lines, and that such authority was understood to derive from Christ himself, who had handed it over to the apostles and their successors in church office.

The classic New Testament text conferring authority to forgive sins is, of course, John 20:19–23. The strategic placement of this resurrection appearance—the risen Lord's first meeting with the apostles on Easter evening—presents forgiveness as the heart of salvation, our entrance into new life. First, the disciples themselves must be forgiven. As Jesus shows them his hands and his side, allowing them to inspect the consequences of sin, including their own cowardly desertion of him, the customary greeting of "shalom" becomes a declaration of pardon: "Peace be with you." So essential is this implied absolution that Jesus says it twice. Released from the burden of guilt, the apostles move from fear into joy: "then the disciples rejoiced when they saw the Lord." Then Jesus invokes his own apostolic mission from the Father and hands it over to them. In a gesture that recalls God's breathing life into the inanimate Adam of the creation story, the Risen Christ also sets a new creation in motion. He breathes the Holy Spirit into his disciples, and by this he releases into the world the possibility of forgiveness: "'Peace be with you. As the Father has sent me, so I send you.' When he had said this, he breathed on them and said to them, 'Receive the Holy Spirit. If you forgive the sins of any, they are forgiven them; if you retain the sins of any, they are retained.'" To encounter the risen Christ is to find, unexpectedly, forgiveness and peace.

In this way the various strands of evidence in the New Testament point to a spectrum of pastoral approaches to reconciliation within the incipient church. Unlike the formulae for baptism or the Lord's Supper, however, the church did not inherit any clear tradition for ritually enacting forgiveness on behalf of penitent Christians. The most common way Christians would have sought divine forgiveness for everyday lapses would have been through prayer, both personal and corporate. The daily use of the Lord's Prayer, with its petition for forgiveness, and the practice of mutual confession of sin among Christians, offered quietly and in private as well as in public communal gatherings, would have been the norm. St. Paul, after all, had enjoined self-examination prior to coming to the Lord's table, and the *Didache* describes a form of confession practiced among Christians as preparatory to sharing the eucharistic meal.

With the sporadic outbreak of persecution of the church in the second and third centuries, the issue of reconciling those who had abandoned the faith under pressure became urgent. Although there were at first some who, like the authors of Hebrews and 1 John, regarded apostasy as outside the scope of the church's power to forgive, eventually the church devised a means of absolving those who had once abandoned the faith but later sought restoration. Just as baptism drove a wedge between one's former life of sin and the new life of grace, so the developing practice of formal reconciliation required drastic renunciations and severe penances, often lasting for years and even decades. Those who had committed the grave sins of murder and adultery were included with the apostates in this course of penance and absolution, but in the case of the two former sins, which were capital crimes under Roman law, the penance might be performed secretly.

The first step in the process entailed a voluntary private confession of sin, usually made to the bishop, although occasionally he would designate certain presbyters to receive such confessions. On the basis of the confession, a penance was assigned proportionate to the sin. Penitents were excluded from communion, ritually dismissed at the same time as the catechumens at the conclusion of the Liturgy of the Word. From their place at the back of the church or by its doors, they would beg for prayers from the faithful as they entered the church. Other aspects of penitential ritual included dressing in rags or sackcloth, prostrations before the clergy, and the bishop's prayers over the penitential group. During the period of excommunication, the bishop would make regular pastoral calls on penitents, encouraging them to persevere in their penance and embrace the demands of a Christian life. When the bishop deemed the penitent ready and the congregation satisfied that sufficient penance had been performed, he would restore the penitent to communion with prayer and a solemn laying-on-of-hands. This ceremony usually took place just before Easter on either Maundy Thursday or Holy Saturday. For any individual penitent, such an avenue to restoration was available only once.

These public penitential rites of the patristic era provided a way forward for the church to reconcile Christians guilty of serious sin, while driving home for penitents and congregants alike the enormity of it. Yet their severity caused problems for the church, too. Many people postponed penance until late—or too late—in life for the same reason people put off baptism; they had a healthy skepticism about their capacity to measure up to the rigors of this discipline or were unwilling even to try. So in the western church, especially after large numbers of northern tribes were admitted to baptism without the careful and thorough catechumenate of earlier days, public rites of penance gradually faded away. Recently scholars have documented some diversity in forms of public or quasi-public penance in certain regions of Europe up to the thirteenth century.[7] But for the most part, public rituals of penance were reserved for heinous crimes or high-profile offenders such as emperors and kings.

Fortunately, another means of spiritual unburdening developed side by side with public ecclesiastical penance. This was the private confession of sin to a mature and wise Christian, whether lay or ordained,

---

7 Rob Meens, "The Historiography of Early Medieval Penance," in *A New History of Penance*, ed. Abigail Firey (Leiden and Boston: Brill, 2008), 73–95.

to seek that person's prayer, encouragement, and counsel. It was in the monastic movement, begun in the deserts of Egypt, Syria, and Palestine, that this custom became widespread. What was confided to a monk or nun of holy reputation was a wide-ranging "disclosure of thoughts"— not merely sinful actions or words, but the whole gamut of troublesome thoughts and feelings that disturbed the soul. In the intense solitude of monastic life, such self-disclosure was immensely healing, and the guidance provided in these encounters fostered spiritual growth and insight. The sixth-century Rule of St. Benedict incorporated the desert practice of disclosure of thoughts when it counseled, "As soon as wrongful thoughts come into your heart, dash them against Christ and disclose them to your spiritual father" (Rule of Benedict 4:50). Thus a form of private confession entered the burgeoning monastic enterprise.

It was through the influence of Celtic Christianity that the shift to private confession became the norm. The Celtic churches of Britain and Ireland were so remote from the Roman world that they developed in ways markedly different from the churches around the Mediterranean. It is not clear how Christianity first came to this region, but the monastic movement rapidly gave the church its unique form and character. It was typically organized along tribal lines, with monastic settlements as the centers of Christian life. The public penances of the Mediterranean world seem to have been unknown; instead, the kind of private confession fostered in monastic circles prevailed, usually made to a lay "soul friend." Confession was often intertwined with what we would call spiritual direction, just as it had been for the desert ascetics. Over time, as the practice of private confession was brought to continental Europe, aspects of the Celtic and Mediterranean traditions became fused. Confession was made privately, as in Britain and Ireland, but to a bishop or priest, as in the earlier ecclesiastical discipline. The role of the priest was further enhanced when the bishop's authority of the keys "to bind and loose" was transferred (as were many other prerogatives of the earliest bishops) to priests. After both serious and lighter sins were confessed, the priest would assign a penance to be performed. After its faithful completion, however long that might take, absolution was pronounced.

One regrettable legacy of both the patristic and the Celtic traditions was the tendency to make the performance of penance—prayer, fasting, and other physical austerities—the focal point of reconciliation. Although initially seen as a token of sincere repentance and a means of combating temptation, the practice of penance ended up becoming the heart of the matter. A distinct form of pastoral literature, called "penitentials," spread abroad by the Celtic church, exacerbated this tendency. Penitentials were handbooks designed to help confessors assign appropriate penances for sins, and while some distinctions were made based upon the actual situation of penitents and their motivations, on the whole these handbooks presented a fairly rigid scheme of what penances fit which sin. More troubling still was the incorporation of aspects of tribal law, which allowed for the payment of tariffs for offenses (as under civil law) and even vicarious penance, whereby the penitent could hire someone else to perform it. In this way the practice became almost wholly external. Emanating initially from the Irish church, these penitentials were copied and imitated on the European continent and among Anglo-Saxon Christians. Although they differed markedly from each other in their prescriptions and lacked any official ecclesiastical backing, penitentials became enormously popular, especially with poorly educated clergy who could look to them for guidance in their role as confessors. Yet the emphasis on penance, with its implication that forgiveness might be earned by making sufficient "satisfaction" for sin, was a theological time-bomb waiting for the Reformation to explode.

The benefit of confession as a ministry of renewal, healing, and comfort, however, was by no means lost in the Middle Ages. Writing at the end of the eighth century, the learned deacon Alcuin of York affirmed sacerdotal authority to bind and loose in confession, while interpreting this aspect of priestly ministry as a distinctive feature of the cure of souls. "The ministry of the physician will come to an end if the sick do not lay bare their wounds," he wrote in one of his letters, urging the exposure of spiritual ills through confession. The medical analogy was a frequent theme in the literature on confession, appearing earlier in the Venerable Bede and later in scholastic theologians such as Abelard and Aquinas.[8] Further salutary developments had taken place by the eleventh century. By then a more "streamlined" penitential rite meant that absolution would be pronounced right at the conclusion of the confession rather than requiring penitents to wait until they had performed their penance. This had the constructive effect of shifting the weight of significance to contrition and absolution rather than acts of reparation. During this period private confession had become sufficiently normative in the western church that in 1215 the Fourth Lateran Council required an annual confession to one's own priest by all those who had come to "the years of discretion." This same decree made reception of Holy Communion during the Easter season similarly binding, and these regulations continue to be in effect in the Roman Catholic Church to this day.

Because the issue of personal salvation was at the center of much Reformation controversy, sacramental confession came under exacting scrutiny and heated debate. First, there was the question of its sacramental status. While today we allow for the evolution of sacramental rites in the church over time, we must remember that historical awareness was in its infancy at the Reformation. Most reformers argued that since auricular confession had not been instituted by Christ, it could not be regarded as a sacrament of the church, nor was it necessary for salvation. Confession should therefore never be compulsory. Moreover, they insisted that neither contrition nor penance earned forgiveness because salvation is an utterly free gift received by faith in Christ.

Luther, however, maintained a high regard for the practice of confession to bring relief to the individual conscience, and he continued to

8 Martin Dudley, "The Sacrament of Penance in Catholic Teaching and Practice," in *Confession and Absolution*, 58–59.

make his own confession throughout his life.[9] He sometimes spoke of it as the "third sacrament," although he regarded confession to be but an aspect of baptism. For him, Christian discipleship entailed a daily living out of baptism—that is, a daily mortification or death to sin. Other continental reformers were fierce in their denunciations not only of abuses, but of confession itself. Zwingli viewed it, at most, as a form of pastoral consultation; Calvin set confession aside as a sacrament, but recognized the value of unburdening the conscience to one's pastor in order to receive the consolation of the gospel. Writing as a pastoral theologian, Martin Bucer took yet another route, relocating confession in Protestant practice as a feature of home visitation. Thus the faithful pastor was charged "to assist people in their personal lives of faith at the point where sin, especially habitual sin, had to be brought to repentance and life amended."[10] Moreover, the continental reformers affirmed the "power of the keys" as a means both of maintaining church order and absolving penitent sinners. For that reason the Lutheran *Shorter Catechism* and the Westminster Assembly of 1643 endorsed confession to a pastor, followed by absolution.[11]

The English reformers made provision for a reformed understanding and practice of confession, making explicit liturgical references to it. In the first English Book of Common Prayer (1549), the Exhortation in the service of Holy Communion concludes by encouraging those whose consciences were troubled to make "secret confession" to a priest. The same prayer book directed that the absolution specified in the Visitation to the Sick also be used for "all private confessions." That absolution, based on the Sarum Manual, was repeated in the 1662 Book of Common Prayer and is substantially the form for absolution in the rites for private confession in the Australian (1978),

9 Thomas N. Tentler, *Sin and Confession on the Eve of the Reformation* (Princeton: Princeton University Press, 1977), 349.
10 Andrew Purves, "A Confessing Faith: Assent and Penitence in the Reformation Traditions of Luther, Calvin, and Bucer," in *Repentance in Christian Tradition*, ed. Mark J. Boda and Gordon T. Smith (Collegeville, MN: Liturgical Press, 2006), 260.
11 Geoffrey Rowell, "The Anglican Tradition: From the Reformation to the Oxford Movement," in *Confession and Absolution*, 91–92.

American (1979), Welsh (1984), and South African (1989) prayer books; it is also one of the absolutions provided in *Common Worship* of the Church of England (2006). In the course of Anglican history, use of private confession has waxed and waned along with other aspects of sacramental life. But it has never entirely disappeared, and the liturgical renewal of recent decades, which has given it a full rite in many prayer books, has lifted the practice out of obscurity and made it more available than ever. We do not need to turn to scholastic arguments or Reformation controversies to recognize that rites of reconciliation, as palpable vehicles of the divine mercy entrusted by Christ to his church, mediate sacramental grace. The fact that over time the church evolved diverse ways of conveying the forgiveness of sin is only to be expected, since the Holy Spirit works in and through history.

The General Confession

The relationship of private confession to the General Confession and Absolution must be clarified so that the one does not seem to undermine the other. The Book of Common Prayer, like most reformed liturgies, provided for a General Confession and Absolution.[12] This was a decidedly pastoral strategy, since the reformers perceived that Christian people would continue to need some way to acknowledge their sinfulness and be absolved once private confession was no longer required. The presence of the General Confession and Absolution in our liturgies significantly shapes our Christian identity. Like other penitential prayers, it presses home our baptismal renunciation of sin, while offering assurance of forgiveness through Christ. Because the General Confession is a corporate prayer, moreover, its primary role is to articulate the sinful failings of the community *as community*. It understands that we remain a sinful people, entangled in the destructive forces at work in our fallen

---

12 Marion J. Hatchett, in his *Commentary on the American Prayer Book* (New York: Seabury Press, 1981), 341, notes that at the end of the Middle Ages, priest and server exchanged a mutual confession and absolution prior to the Mass, but that a confession of sin on the part of the entire congregation was an innovation of the Reformation.

world, compromised in many ways. As the American pastoral theologian Andrew Purves writes:

> In an interdependent world repentance/penance has a special complexity, perhaps. A person's complicity in sin is magnified exponentially, for example (and the point, of course, is political), by virtue of medications and cosmetics tested on live animals, clothes made under labor practices that would not be tolerated in the United States, and disproportionate use of the world's natural resources. Much of the time we might even be quite unaware of our accommodation to social and economic sin, when our benefits and apparent blessings are obtained unknowingly in the context of exploitation of others. In a world such as this, repentance/penance surely means deepening economic and political awareness. The concept of a faithful penitential life is expanded to be a life of solidarity with and working for the benefit of the "least of them." A penitential life may well come to mean the practice of pious suspicion.[13]

Because our common life is shot through with common sin, both known and unknown, we need to hear the liberating words of absolution. Amendment of life, in the case of social sin, demands practicing Purves' "pious suspicion" about the real cost—human and environmental—of our benefits and privileges, coupled with a determination to reduce the harm we have caused to whatever extent we can.

Yet the reach of the absolution pronounced after the General Confession is not restricted to our social and corporate sins; it covers our personal sins as well. Especially for those who come to the liturgy burdened with remembrance of particular sins, the words of the

---

13 Andrew Purves, "A Confessing Faith," 265.

General Confession are roomy enough to find a place, at least in a general way, for them. By regularly confronting us with the reality of our sinfulness and the grace of divine forgiveness, its frequent use can help prevent us from turning into the sort of "pious fellowship" we discussed earlier, one that "permits no one to be a sinner."

However, the General Confession and Absolution suffers from some real limitations, especially today. For many people, the repetition of a generic confession week after week simply loses its force over time. The impact of the declarations of forgiveness given in the liturgy thus becomes weaker and weaker, while the bland language of contemporary penitential rites exacerbates this problem. To acknowledge that we have not loved God "with our whole heart" or "our neighbors as ourselves" makes little claim on us, and such a mild admission of imperfection hardly elicits true compunction of heart. Yet the move in some quarters to flesh out the General Confession with more specific sins usually winds up as a narrow, ideologically driven litany of offenses. Once again, we seem to be mouthing sins for which we feel no sense of personal conviction; and confessing them, far from moving us towards repentance, instead reinforces self-righteousness.

The power of this form of confession has also lost ground because of the excessively reassuring environment of most liberal churches, where the fact of subjective guilt and the cost of discipleship are often ignored. In many places, the judgment theme of the gospels has been reduced to nil, and sacramental hospitality has been distorted into cheap grace. Much preaching offers no real summons to self-examination and repentance, and people are encouraged to approach the eucharist with no expectation of commitment to Christ. When we are not specifically taught how to examine our consciences, we are left with some pretty rudimentary understandings of sin. Hence our capacity for sincere repentance never gets developed, and the absolution offered in the liturgy is reduced to another comforting noise. However, because the disabling guilt from which we actually suffer is still there, all the well-meaning affirmation begins to feel hollow.

Clearly, some of these shortcomings could be rectified by more authentically evangelical preaching and a well-grounded catechesis of children and adults, including attention to spiritual formation. The renunciations and affirmations of the baptismal liturgy need to be fully explained, along with the creeds and commitments of the baptismal covenant, as the basis of Christian spirituality and our common life. The upshot of a renewed context for the General Confession and Absolution might be twofold: it could lead to a fresh grasp of the power of the penitential rites in the liturgy, and it might foster the desire to experience, in a more personal and powerful way, the grace of God's forgiveness.

Distinctive Benefits of the Rite of Reconciliation

Reconciliation stands at the center of the gospel proclamation. St. Paul declares that "in Christ God was reconciling the world to himself, not counting their trespasses against them, and entrusting the message of reconciliation to us" (2 Corinthians 5:19). Furthermore, God takes the initiative in the work of reconciliation, restoring communion with those who have become estranged from their Creator. The ministry of reconciliation God, through the church, shares with us extends to the whole of creation and embraces all nations and peoples, bringing Christians to the forefront of witness for justice and peace. Yet Christians who, because of their baptism into Christ, are ministers of reconciliation, also themselves stand in need of reconciliation at different points in their lives. Sometimes it takes place on the stage of the world's theater, as in the Truth and Reconciliation Commission of South Africa, headed by Archbishop Desmond Tutu. There participants found that simply telling the truth about what happened during the years of apartheid, admitting what they had done, was wrenching but cathartic. Hearing these confessions of appalling crimes and atrocities was costly, too, especially for the victims and the victims' families. But after years of lies and denials, uncovering the truth was deeply healing.

For most of us, the experience of reconciliation with others is usually less dramatic but often no less powerful—an apology offered decades after an injury; a humble admission of wrongdoing or insensitivity by a family member, friend, or colleague; the restitution of property or reputation; or simply yielding up in prayer a painful memory. We also serve as ministers of reconciliation when we bear one another's burdens, whether of sadness, loss, or guilt. The re-embracing love of God, and the taking away of sin by Christ crucified, is conveyed by a whole range of ministries of admonishing, consoling, strengthening, uplifting, and encouraging that we carry out in the Christian community. Practical care for others, including teaching or counseling, can help people experience the love of God and gain some freedom from sin.

The church also mediates the grace of Christ when it fosters individual penitential prayer. This is not as easy as it sounds. Western culture has strong defenses in place to resist any admission of wrongdoing, and popular notions of right and wrong are at best superficial and often skewed. In such a climate, embarking on prayers of confession will necessitate some preliminary moral and spiritual reeducation. Much of the training in the three-year catechumenate of the early church was devoted to just such a project, as would-be Christians unlearned the habits and attitudes of pagan antiquity and took on the mind of Christ. Those formed by our own secular, narcissistic, violent, and consumerist culture require a similar deprogramming so they can begin to notice patterns of sin, feel sorrow for them, and seek God's forgiveness in prayer. Since the earliest days of the church, such prayer has been the usual way Christians have confessed their sins and appropriated the gift of forgiveness through faith. However, this way of praying should by no means be construed as an entirely private transaction between the soul and God. All Christian prayer, even the most solitary and secret, takes place within a larger spiritual context: the community of the church, the body of Christ. Our prayer springs up from the action of the Holy Spirit who animates the church and dwells in the recesses of our hearts. All prayer, like all sin, has social repercussions.

While granting the sufficiency of all these channels of reconciliation, the church recognizes that they are not exhaustive. Some people need or desire a more compelling vehicle of repentance and forgiveness, and the rite of the Reconciliation of a Penitent exists for just this purpose. It is also available for those who readily benefit from all the other ways we experience reconciliation in the church, yet want to reach out for the maximum help in the struggles of ongoing conversion. As a burning glass concentrates the rays of the sun in a single point, sacramental confession focuses contrition and absolution with searing intensity.

With its extensive roots in the formal canonical penance of the first millennium, in the disclosure of thoughts of monastic practice, and in the sacrament of penance of the Middle Ages, the Anglican approach to sacramental confession is distinguished by its pastoral emphasis. This is true as well for other reformed churches—Lutherans, Presbyterians, and the United Church of Christ—which today offer rites for individual confession and pardon. Confession is not required: "All may, none must, some should" declares the familiar Anglican adage. It still holds. The Exhortation contained in the 1549 Book of Common Prayer had urged that the "rule of charity" inform diversity of practice with regard to private confession. The excellent Preface to the rites of Confession and Absolution in the South African Book of Common Prayer repeats this admonition:

> Those who are satisfied with a private confession to God in prayer ought not to be offended with those who use confession to God in the presence of a priest; nor ought those who think it necessary to confess their sins in the presence of a priest be offended with those who are satisfied with their confession to God in prayer together with the general confession of the Church. All should remember to follow and keep the

rule of love and not to judge other people's conscience since there is no warrant for this in God's word.

There are several distinct yet related reasons why people seek the sacramental rite of confession. For instance, some people believe in divine mercy but rarely, if ever, experience it: for them forgiveness seems to exist only in the realm of ideas. And it is a weak form of ministry, when people feel blocked in accepting forgiveness, to suggest that they merely change their thinking. Many of us need some way of dramatizing and exteriorizing what we are feeling in order to change and evolve. The rite of reconciliation fills this gap, shifting forgiveness from the head into a heartfelt appropriation of penitence and joy. "You have shown yourself to me face to face, O Christ: I meet you in your sacraments," wrote St. Ambrose of Milan. The experience of Ambrose has been repeated millions of times, as people encounter Christ in the sacraments, particularly in the intimate yet corporate communion of the eucharist. Yet the Risen Lord ministers to our specific needs in each sacrament of the church. Through confession and absolution Christ is present as our merciful savior, and contact with him is transformative. The recovery of this sacramental rite, along with the renewal of the healing ministry of the church in the prayer book ritual of Anointing and Laying on of Hands, is part of the restoration of incarnational spirituality instead of what could be a private, rationalistic piety.

Because the sacraments are rooted in the human experience of time, they work as rites of passage, enacting the transition from one phase of life to another. As a single event in time, moreover, the rite of reconciliation can act as a milestone on the Christian journey, closing off the past and marking the commencement of a new stage. With the private prayer of penitence there is not always such an unambiguous before-and-after as there is with the celebration of a sacramental rite. This holds true even for those who regularly use confession, for whom it might not signal a dramatic turning point. Something clear and definite happens in the rite, and the dismissal at the end always inaugurates a fresh start.

Confession also helps us be specific in our repentance. Many people are weighed down by vague feelings of guilt or remorse, with some carrying shameful memories for decades. Others sense that they are somehow inadequate as spouses, partners, or parents, or "not as charitable as I ought to be." The responsibility of spelling out our sins in confession counteracts our tendency to be fuzzy and general in our penitence. Preparation for confession (discussed in chapter three) can be an enormous help in itself. Honest and thorough self-examination might lead us to discard obsolete images of ourselves—those stories about ourselves that we have been inwardly repeating for years. False notions of guilt and self-blame can be set aside, and real responsibility for our omissions and transgressions taken up. Because in confession we need to make ourselves intelligible to another person, we have to cut to the chase and own up to what we have done and not done, painstakingly finding the words to name our particular sins. We commit ourselves to being comprehensive and straightforward. Since all Christians have a duty to practice regular self-examination and repent of their sins, preparing for confession can spur us on to be focused and intentional in doing it. As a result we can move past the blur of hazy guilt feelings to a sharp and liberating penitence.

Modern life can sometimes be so complex that more and more of us are confused about what is right and wrong in our lives. This is the situation envisioned in the Exhortation, a very pastoral text that emphasizes the importance of authentic repentance in all those coming to the eucharistic meal and speaks compassionately of those who get stuck in their preparation. Christians can become baffled and thwarted because they cannot tell whether certain aspects of their lives are benign and acceptable or run counter to God's will, and this dilemma can only become more common as life becomes more complicated. People may find it hard to unravel the threads of their precise responsibility in knotty situations in which no solution seemed workable or right at the time. The rite of reconciliation provides a means of getting help in distinguishing what in our life calls for repentance and forgiveness and what does not. It also creates a suitable setting in which to receive specific guidance and counsel about our particular struggle with sin. As long as we keep our sins to ourselves, we have to rely on the general preaching addressed to everyone from the pulpit or in whatever reading we may do on our own. These means of grace are valuable and can be enlightening, but not always; they may also lead us to deceive ourselves. Disclosing our sins in confession allows our pastor to speak specifically and directly to our condition.

Left to our own devices, there is often room for doubt about what we may be experiencing in prayer: Are we actually in touch with the forgiveness of God, or merely letting ourselves off too easily? Are we just fooling ourselves about our repentance and desire to amend? Sometimes it can be difficult to tell whether we are merely exonerating ourselves or receiving real pardon. The Exhortation cites the "removal of scruple and doubt" (BCP, 317) as one of the advantages of private confession, for the rite of reconciliation breaks through these doubts. In the words of absolution we receive an objective, authoritative assurance of God's forgiveness. It is not our own little voice that we hear inside our heads, but the voice of someone authorized to speak on behalf of Christ and his church. Absolution is pronounced in response to our confessed sins and no one else's; it applies the mercy of God directly to our circumstances.

Confession brings destructive secrets into the open. There exists a profound human need to express our vulnerability and articulate our guilt, yet we shy away from it. It is tempting to deny and hide, even from ourselves, the shadowy, damaged side of ourselves. Our familiarity with psychotherapy has prepared a generation that can appreciate the wisdom of the church's provision of a place to tell the truth about the pained and troubled self, and its loveless and harmful behaviors. The ancient practice of "disclosure of thoughts," even the darkest and most shameful, was grounded in this shrewd understanding of human nature. The biblical connection between confession of sin and healing takes on new meaning. While we no longer see sickness as a punishment for sin, we do know more than ever how toxic are the weight of unforgiven sin and the wounds of unhealed memories. Taking their toll on body and soul, they are a contributing factor to all sorts of ill health. Saying our sins out loud makes them real to us and deepens our penitence. At the same time, it helps us unburden ourselves and hand these sins over to the mercy of God. Pent up, anguishing memories are released as we communicate them to another and let them go. Admitting our long-concealed sins and deceptions, as the ailing family does in the final scenes of *Mercy Me*, frees us from their tyranny and enables us to reconstruct even our sense of the past.

Still, the rite of reconciliation, while therapeutic, is not psychotherapy on the cheap. It is a sacrament, an encounter with Christ through the ministry of the church, and its purpose is the forgiveness of sin. By the grace of God, forgiveness is itself healing, and the whole process of contrition, confession, amendment, and absolution is restorative. After confession, we are apt to feel like the Gerasene demoniac in the aftermath of his deliverance by Jesus: freed of his compulsions and demons, the man is reinstated among the living, calm, and returned to his "right mind" (Mark 5:15). Moreover, this rite by which God forgives, heals, and reconciles us to himself is grounded in the guarantee that what is disclosed in confession will be held in the strictest confidentiality. In the Church of England, Canon 113 of 1604 enforced the longstanding discipline of the seal of confession and made it binding on all who hear confessions. As *Common Worship* observes, it is one of the few ancient canons that is still binding today. The seal of confession is absolute and permits of no exceptions whatsoever. It means that people can approach this sacrament feeling secure that their sins will not be disclosed or their revelations abused. Other provinces of the Anglican Communion as well as other churches that offer individual reconciliation have similar provisions in place.

Above all, sacramental confession offers a vigorous renewal of baptism. From the first, the church's rites of reconciliation were interpreted as an extension of the "one baptism for the forgiveness of sins," as the Nicene Creed puts it. It liturgically enacts our dying to sin and rising to new life in Christ in a rite that generates a forceful interior appropriation of this twofold movement of grace. Since baptism immerses us into Christ's death, the forgiveness of sins will bring about a fresh exposure to the cross of Christ. It is hard to reveal our sins to a priest because it goes against the grain of our concern with self-image. It means taking off a mask, exposing our fallibility and hurt and our capacity to hurt others. The costly self-exposure we undergo in confession means we participate in the costliness of the cross. Forgiveness comes at a steep price; it is not a casual affair. What is more, death to sin requires letting go of the destructive mechanisms we have put in place to cope with life's pains and injustices; it involves relinquishing a false identity to "put on Christ" instead. Confession undermines one of the deepest roots of sin, which is pride. In *Life Together*, Bonhoeffer trenchantly expresses this severe grace:

> In confession occurs the break-through to the Cross . . .
> I want to be my own law, I have a right to myself, my
> hatred and my desires, my life and my death. . . . Con-
> fession in the presence of a brother is the profoundest
> kind of humiliation. It hurts, it cuts a man down, it
> is a dreadful blow to pride. To stand there before a
> brother as a sinner is an ignominy that is almost
> unbearable. In the confession of concrete sins the old
> man dies a painful, shameful death before the eyes of
> a brother.[14]

Then, in the pause between the penitent's confession of sin and the words of the priest, a significant shift occurs. The death to sin, insofar

---

14 *Life Together*, 113–114.

as we can accomplish it, has been completed for now. Our trouble is not analyzed or probed but surrounded by healing words of encouragement and grace. However succinctly, the gospel is proclaimed and applied to us. We are not overwhelmed with our guilt since the rite enacts our handing it over to Christ, the Lamb of God who takes away the sin of the world. The deep catharsis of confession is ratified by the words of absolution. From the unfathomable creativity of resurrection life, the Risen Christ imparts forgiveness, and his Spirit breathes new life into us. Joy springs up and we are anchored in hope.

Experiencing a renewal of baptismal grace through the rite of reconciliation reinforces the truth that we sin and are forgiven as members of the community of Christ. Sin can make us excruciatingly lonely: public sins can estrange our neighbors from us, while hidden sins can estrange us from them. In reconciliation we reach out to the church through the person of a priest, and our isolation is overcome.

Although the term "private confession" helpfully distinguishes it from the general confession of public liturgy, the term can also be misleading. It can give the impression that sacramental confession is not a regular ministry of the church, but an odd devotional practice for the exceptionally pious or a therapeutic support for the notoriously sinful. But although this rite requires "privacy," still, as in all sacramental actions, the whole church is gathered for worship in the presence of the Lord. In this case, the smallest quorum of the church is at hand: "Where two or three are gathered in my name, there I am in the midst of them." *The Book of Alternative Services* of the Anglican Church of Canada sums up the true character of the rite clearly: "The Reconciliation of a Penitent, although private, is a corporate action of the church because sin affects the unity of the Body. The absolution is restoration to full fellowship: the priest declares the forgiveness which Christ has invested in his Church." Reconciliation with God in Christ and reconciliation with the community are bound up together.

Yet many priests and pastors hear confessions only rarely, if ever. In many mainstream parishes the practice of confession might be entirely unknown or regarded with suspicion as a borrowing from Roman Catholicism. The renewal of sacramental and liturgical life in the church, however, and the incorporation of rites of reconciliation into Anglican prayer books, has gradually helped to bring the practice of confession out of the shadows and into the open. Meanwhile, there is much teaching to be done. If clergy never mention sacramental confession, their congregations quickly pick up the cue: "We don't do that here." Although it would be false to Christian freedom and contrary to the pastoral accent of Anglicanism ever to pressure people into confession, still their range of choice is severely limited if they do not even know it exists for them! Instruction about the theology and practice of reconciliation, along with the Anointing and Laying on of Hands, should be part of every confirmation, inquirers', and basic catechesis class. Today the traditional Exhortation is seldom heard in our churches, although the simple practice of using it one Sunday during the seasons of Advent and Lent to begin the penitential rite would acquaint our congregations with its pastoral message. Advent and Lent, along with other occasions furnished by the lectionary, also present timely opportunities to preach on repentance and forgiveness.

Pastoral preachers know how to connect this central gospel topic both with their congregation's lives and the church's liturgical practice. Most people could benefit from some coaching about how to approach the General Confession and Absolution, as could many who are unaware of the rite of reconciliation. While whole sermons do not have to be devoted to these subjects, the conjunction of personal repentance with liturgical expression should be explored from time to time. By these means and others that arise in the course of pastoral ministry, we can make known Christ's gift of forgiveness through the church. Simply talking sympathetically and intelligently about sacramental confession lessens the atmosphere of fearsome mystique or mocking humor that surrounds it in some quarters. As theologian Kenneth

Leech observed some years ago, "Confession is a way of making systematic and effective the essential struggle against evil that is so central to the life in Christ. It is not an abnormal, crisis activity, but is part of the day-by-day, domestic ministry of the church."[15] It is a ministry of pastors, seeking and finding the lost sheep of Christ.

15 Kenneth Leech, *True Prayer: An Invitation to Christian Spirituality* (San Francisco: Harper & Row, 1980), 132.

CHAPTER TWO

"A Wise and Discerning Priest"

Who may serve as a minister of the rite of reconciliation in the church? Both the Canadian and American rites provide a Declaration of Forgiveness to be used by a deacon or lay confessor, while the Irish Book of Common Prayer suggests that a deacon might have recourse to the "Comfortable Words" and a "suitable prayer" after hearing a confession. In these cases the church is giving scope to the practice of making confession to lay people that is undoubtedly part of the tradition, and Christians remain free to confess their sins to any fellow Christian. Still, the rite of reconciliation is most appropriately administered by bishops and priests because they are ordained to act on behalf of the whole church. The ministry of absolution is reserved to them because it is an authoritative action of the church, exercising the power to forgive sin entrusted to it by the Risen Christ. Hearing confessions and pronouncing absolution belongs emphatically to the cure of souls.

If hearing confessions is part of the day-to-day ministry of the church, then clergy need to reclaim its importance for their pastoral vocation. It is not a fringe ministry for a few priests who "do that sort of thing." Although the hours spent in hearing confessions may be few compared with those devoted to other responsibilities, our attitude towards this ministry has bearing on our larger sense of vocation. After all, Anglican ordination rites speak of the ministry of absolution as a distinctive charge given to priests, and some ordinals include the words of John 20: 22–23—"Whose sins you forgive, they are forgiven; whose sins you retain, they are retained"—as the bishop lays hands on the ordinand. The authority to forgive sins in the name of Christ is an explicit priestly responsibility, named along with preaching, teaching, blessing, pastoral oversight, and the celebration of the sacraments. The vocation of the priest lies precisely in this unique constellation of ministries, each aspect of which is essential to the calling. In the course of their work, priests discover to their joy how every dimension of this many-sided vocation is permeated by every other. Preaching, for instance, is not an isolated lecture, but speech grounded in the celebration of the liturgy, informed by pastoral care, and shaped by the rhythms of the liturgical year. Pastoral counsel, even when in strictest confidentiality, is still offered within the community of the church, conditioned by her faith, worship, fellowship, and eschatological horizon. Examples of the way the threads of priestly vocation intertwine are endless.

However, in recent years these related aspects of one integrated pastoral ministry have suffered fragmentation. Particular ministries have spun off from this central core into ministerial specializations, most notably the related ministries of spiritual direction, pastoral counseling, and confession. Of course, some clergy are bound to have more of their time engaged in these ministries than in others. But a problem arises when regular parish clergy consider themselves unprepared for these classic pastoral tasks or even imagine themselves exempt from their exercise. The cure of souls has, oddly enough, become a niche ministry.

The Ministry of Spiritual Direction

Spiritual direction—now fairly widespread in our churches—is one facet of the cure of souls, offered over a long space of time to certain individuals. Yet the revival of spiritual direction has allowed some priests to think they are excused from providing spiritual guidance to their parishioners, because they have come to think of it as a ministry for a few specially trained experts. In itself, of course, the resurgence of spiritual direction since the 1970s has been a welcome sign of vitality in the church. Both clergy and lay people have received and offered this ministry in increasing numbers. With roots in the ancient ministry of "discernment of spirits," spiritual direction seeks to deepen the relation to God. Of course, this is the goal of all authentic Christian ministry, but spiritual direction works through pastoral conversation to help people notice how and where God has been present and active in their lives. Many people have profound intuitions of God that they discount or repress, often for fear of being misunderstood. Spiritual direction encourages people to speak of their experience of God as part of the ordinary life of discipleship. The Holy Spirit dwells in our hearts, constantly influencing us. But in the press, turmoil, or monotony of our daily lives, we can easily miss this divine guidance or find ourselves confused by ambiguous evidence. Spiritual direction works by discernment to clarify our situation with God as it unfolds in our day-to-day lives so we may respond more readily to grace.

Already in the New Testament we see evidence of the need for discernment in the life of the community. The first letter of John advises: "Test the spirits to see whether they are from God" (4:1). Human beings, after all, are subject to all sorts of pressures. Some promptings of a rather neutral sort may spring simply from our psychological or physical makeup. Others may arise from the gentle or firm nudging of the Holy Spirit, moving us to deeper faithfulness to God, closer union with Christ, and service to others. Still others, typically disguised as something else, may lead us away from God and into personal or communal disintegration. All these spiritual currents are embedded in the particular contours of our lives. By careful and prayerful listening, informed by the spiritual wisdom of the church, spiritual directors help people notice how God may be present to them in previously overlooked ways. They might also observe how unrealistic, self-defeating, or deceptive undercurrents may be subtly at work.

As a ministry oriented towards ongoing maturity in Christ, spiritual direction resembles the ministry of hearing confessions in that neither one is meant to be psychotherapy. Consequently it does not aim to mend deep psychic wounds, but rather to enhance someone's relation to God. To be sure, crises have a way of cropping up in the course of every life, but spiritual direction does not seek so much to solve problems as to interpret difficulties in relationship to the gospel. As a faithful pastor, the spiritual director tries to enter empathetically into the directee's situation while holding it in the light of Christ. Although healing at various levels may, and often does, occur over time, it is not the sole purpose of spiritual direction. What distinguishes it from other forms of pastoral counseling is, above all, its duration—once in place, this relationship may continue for months and even years.

Nowadays most dioceses discourage or forbid clergy to engage in extended counseling relationships, and this is a prudent and sensible precaution. Most clergy do not have the requisite skills, and the amateur exercise of "pastoral counseling" is dangerous. The basic training seminarians undergo, including clinical pastoral education, is instead geared towards developing fluency in the sort of conversations parish priests and chaplains have in the course of their work. It is valuable to learn how to ask non-threatening questions, be better listeners, or assist people with ordinary difficulties, especially when these skills are practiced over time. Combined with a bit of common sense and life experience, it is astonishing how helpful this can sometimes be! But we also need to know our limitations. While parishioners will often come first to a trusted priest with their personal, relational, or emotional problems, the wise pastor will recognize the complexity of the situation and make a responsible professional referral, usually after one or two meetings. Clergy who have been schooled as psychotherapists can, of course, offer professional help, but in this case they serve in the role of therapist rather than priest or deacon.

Interestingly enough, the rule forbidding extended counseling relationships does not apply to spiritual direction precisely because it does not claim to be professional counseling. The infrequency of its meetings, typically at monthly or longer intervals, also stands in marked contrast to therapeutic counseling and helps protect it from confusion with any form of therapy. For spiritual direction is simply the exercise of ordinary pastoral ministry at a certain depth. All pastors are called to accompany people in their spiritual journeys, helping them interpret the signposts along the way. When parishioners seek us out to discuss a problem, talk about an impending life change, register a theological query, or wonder how prayer could become more real to them, the opportunity for spiritual growth is there. Nothing separates us from the love of God in Christ, and in pastoral conversations clergy are well situated to help people see how the very mundane details of their lives are conspiring to bring them closer to God. We can ask questions in such a way that people might begin to notice how grace (what leads us to God) and temptation (what leads us away) might be at work. The challenge of our baptismal promises is usually lurking just under the surface of everyday events: the occasion to renounce evil in its diverse manifestations and hold fast to Christ.

Yet many pastors, deciding that they are not "spiritual directors," avoid these pastoral openings. They fail to pick up the cues that might lead to engagement at the level of the Spirit or refer people to a spiritual director whenever the least question of spiritual practice comes up in discussion. However, even chance encounters can lead to a brief yet significant exchange. Presbyterian pastor Duane Bidwell describes one such meeting with a stranger on a hospital elevator:

One Sunday evening I took communion to a parishioner in the hospital. As I waited for the elevator, a woman pointed to the communion set and asked, "Bringing the Eucharist to someone?" I nodded. "That's good," she said as we got on the elevator. "Communion is important. I always ask for communion when I'm sick. I don't take it otherwise."

"Why is that?" I asked.

"I don't know," she said, punching the button for her floor. "There's just something healing about it. I think that's what the Eucharist is for, really: healing the body and the soul."

"And you only take it when you're sick?" I asked. She nodded.

As we rode in silence, a question formed in my mind. "May I ask you a personal question?" I said. She agreed, and we looked into each other's eyes for a few seconds. "I wonder," I said finally, "if you'd heal in other ways if you took communion even when your body is fine?"

The elevator opened at her floor. She stepped out but used her hand to stop the door from closing. "Why did you ask me that?" she said with a note of curiosity in her voice.

"I don't know," I said. "I just wonder what sort of relationship God wants with you if you always experience communion as healing? I wonder what might happen if you came home for supper a little more often."

Tears came to her eyes. "I think I just got a hand-delivered invitation," she said. "Supper with my Savior any day I care to stop by." Then she let the elevator doors close.

> In general, I don't recommend (or often practice!) this sort of "hit-and-run" spiritual guidance, but I think my questions served to clarify the woman's disposition towards communion, draw her attention to her experience in the moment, and stimulate reflection on the meaning of her elevator ride with a nosy stranger. With her closing comment, she clearly suggested that she felt God's presence in our conversation.[16]

Bidwell's commentary on this impromptu pastoral moment focuses, appropriately enough, on the woman's situation, but it is worth pondering the pastor's stance as well. While acknowledging that he does not usually practice spur-of-the-moment spiritual guidance, on this occasion Bidwell nonetheless gave himself over to a leading of the Spirit. More than a "nosy stranger," he was in fact keenly aware that he was venturing into sacred territory and showed proper respect for the mystery of this woman's soul. This was conveyed by his polite query, "May I ask you a personal question?" He also framed his insights tentatively, beginning his probing questions to her with "I wonder," recognizing that these proposals needed confirmation from her—they had to ring true. Bidwell "tested the spirits" (in this case, his own interior promptings) and the woman was able to confirm his spiritual hunches because she sensed some corresponding grace stirring within her as they spoke. He took a risk by moving the conversation from somewhat safe religious discourse to press the divine invitation to this particular woman. Like Jesus in his encounter with the Samaritan woman at the well (another "coincidental" meeting), Bidwell shifted the conversation from theological musings to their personal, and possibly uncomfortable, application. In the elevator and by the well, both women discover a sharp, personal grace even as they are drawn out and encouraged by their questioners. One woman finds "living water," and the other "supper with my Savior any day I care to stop by." The pastor's willingness to test and trust

---

16 Duane R. Bidwell, *Short-Term Spiritual Guidance* (Minneapolis: Fortress Press, 2004), 54–55.

the Spirit opened the way for the woman in the elevator to receive a "hand-delivered invitation" from God on the spot. Such moments are a source of grace and thanksgiving for both parties. A pastor's willingness to be used by God in this manner, speaking the divine word directly to another in pastoral conversation, prepares her also to speak it in confession.

Confession and the Pastoral Relationship

Today the ministry of confession usually takes place within an established pastoral relationship. For instance, in the course of a confidential pastoral conversation, a parishioner may disclose a sin or pattern of sinful behavior—a revelation that might begin the conversation or emerge only after a long and difficult exchange. But regardless of how the question of sin comes up in the course of our pastoral work, when someone is mired in guilt or regret and in need of divine forgiveness, we may well feel moved to suggest the rite of reconciliation. If the parishioner has some prior experience with confession, the rite might be celebrated there and then, following the suggestions in chapter three about confession in these circumstances. Or the confession might be made on a later occasion, after the parishioner has had sufficient time to prepare for it.

Some priests are reticent about hearing the confessions of their own parishioners. They feel awkward about meeting them afterwards in social circumstances, conversing with them at the parish coffee hour on Sunday, or working with them on parish committees. Yet pastors regularly "hear confessions," whether sacramentally enacted or not, as part of the ordinary round of parish ministry. We cannot engage in pastoral care without sharing in the messiness of people's lives, including their sin, but we must never leave them there. Proclaiming and enacting the gospel word of forgiveness is central to priestly vocation. If we hesitate to hear our parishioners' confessions, we may be failing to see the rite of reconciliation as a sacrament of liberating grace and joyful new life in Christ, a way of handing over our sin to the mercy of God.

In a few parishes, it is the custom for one or more priests to be available to hear confessions at certain designated hours on a regular basis; in others, such hours may be set aside only during Advent or Lent. Some pastors make a point of bringing into the parish an "external confessor" from time to time in order to enhance their parishioners' choice of confessor. The benefit of offering regularly scheduled hours for confession is that it underscores the ordinariness of using the rite of reconciliation as part of the day-to-day work of the church, thus making it much easier for anyone to come forward and avail themselves of it. In parishes where people have acquired some familiarity with the rite through preaching and teaching, in communities such as seminaries and religious houses, and on conferences and retreats, this ease of access to sacramental reconciliation has much to recommend it.

It would not be wise, however, to offer confession in circumstances in which someone wholly unprepared for the sacrament and unaware of its spiritual demands might attempt to use it. When pastors are asked to hear the confession of a person unknown to them, they should first inquire about the prospective penitent's understanding of the rite and what it entails before going further. Sometimes priests receive telephone calls from desperate souls in search of an understanding ear, or have strangers come to their offices asking for confession. Some of these requests are perfectly appropriate; others come from unstable people seeking, at best, a therapeutic outlet. So it is important to know what is being specifically asked of us before hearing a confession.

In most cases, however, confessions are scheduled simply by making an appointment with the priest. If we have included teaching about reconciliation in our adult and youth classes and spoken about how to schedule a confession, we can expect that some people will seek us out for it. And while we want to be available to hear the confessions of our parishioners, it may be that some of them would prefer another confessor. In that case, we should without hesitation or questioning be ready to refer them to another priest, known to us for skill and experience in administering this sacrament. It may be that certain penitents are referred to us in this same way.

Close pastoral relationships such as spiritual direction often include confession, especially if the director is a priest. While those in spiritual direction, like everyone else, have complete freedom in their choice of confessor, it often seems most natural to them to have the director serve also as the confessor. The frequency of confession would depend upon the individual's preferences. For example, confession might preface or conclude the spiritual direction session, or take place at another time altogether. It is important, however, that confession be set apart from spiritual direction or pastoral conversation with clear, liturgically defined boundaries. Those who wish to separate the ministry of spiritual direction from that of confession should feel free to do so without the least hint of pressure from a priest-director.

The First Step: Being a Penitent

Priests sometimes face particular challenges in finding a confessor or other forms of pastoral care for themselves. Religious and monastic houses often offer a significant ministry to clergy in this respect, but many priests do not live anywhere near such places. Some dioceses have a "chaplain to clergy" who can serve as confessor. Priests who are new to a diocese might inquire about possible confessors and spiritual directors from the bishop, who should be aware of which clergy might best serve in these pastoral roles. Without institutional support or guidance (and many dioceses do not provide much), priests are left to rely on personal recommendations from brother or sister clergy—people whose judgment they have come to trust. This can take time, but it is worth the effort and patience it requires. All clergy need the rite of reconciliation for themselves; without it, they cannot administer it to others.

Some of the reasons for this rule are obvious enough. To begin, there is the issue of professional integrity and competence. Just as the profession of psychology requires therapists to have undergone therapy, so confessors must themselves be penitents. Seeing confession from the penitent's point of view makes one thoroughly accustomed to the rite and sensitive to how it feels. It is unnerving to sense that the priest is inept or uncomfortable through lack of familiarity, and therefore unprepared to coach penitents who may be wondering about either the logistics or the flow of the rite. Penitents should be able to expect that their confessor is wholly conversant with the dynamics of the sacrament and at ease with it.

A correlation also exists between therapy and confession with respect to the self-knowledge acquired by undergoing these healing arts. Both psychological and spiritual maturity depend, in part, on seeing oneself more fully and truthfully. But even beyond the advantages for personal growth, enhanced self-awareness is exceedingly valuable for the future exercise of the office, helping to protect both the therapist and the confessor from the most blatant forms of counter-transference. As priests become increasingly aware of their habitual places of struggle, characteristic failings and blind spots (seen in retrospect), and ingrained attitudes that frustrate and baffle them, they become less likely to impose this interior darkness and confusion on others.

The transparency required for these disciplines is humbling, yet the acute vulnerability needed for either confession or therapy bears fruit in compassion towards others. No one can maintain an Olympian attitude towards the frailties of others after such costly self-exposure. Confession, however, moves beyond the kind of self-knowledge that might be gained through therapy, beneficial as that is, to knowledge of the self in relation with Christ. Dietrich Bonhoeffer, whose own father was a renowned psychiatrist in Berlin, puts the matter this way:

> It is not experience of life but experience of the Cross that makes one a worthy hearer of confessions. The most experienced psychologist or observer of human nature knows infinitely less of the human heart than

the simplest Christian who lives beneath the Cross of
Jesus. . . . In the presence of a psychiatrist I can only
be a sick man; in the presence of a Christian brother I
can dare to be a sinner. . . . Every person should refrain
from listening to confession who does not practice it.
Only the person who has so humbled himself can hear
a brother's confession without harm.[17]

The harm to which Bonhoeffer refers might be injury to either penitent
or confessor. When we make ourselves available to hear confessions, we
must be prepared to encounter the messy, the sinister, and the appalling
without warning. From time to time we are brought very close to real
evil. It requires personal stability and the ability not to be easily shocked
to keep from being undone by it or thrown off balance. In such cases
the grace we have repeatedly received in our own confessions helps prepare us. We know that nothing malicious or foul is entirely alien to us;
the seeds of evil are rooted in our own hearts, whatever our own sinful
actions may or may not have been. What upholds us in these times is
the firm conviction, born out of our experience of divine mercy, that the
Lamb of God alone takes away the sin of the world. In prayer before,
during, and after hearing confessions, we hand the penitent's sins over
to Christ, who bears, absorbs, and finally dissolves them.

By regularly using sacramental confession, we are also grasped by
its joy and become confident of its power. The distinct spiritual challenges that we face as priests perhaps make this particular assurance
especially needful. For instance, it is easy for clergy to feel left out of
the good news they are preaching. We proclaim God's love and forgiveness, yet somehow feel it applies to everyone but ourselves. Sacramental
confession brings the mercy of Christ right into the center of our souls;
it directly addresses our own struggles and failures. And the grace of
absolution given in this setting startles us. We know we did not deserve
it. While Christians rightly hope for forgiveness, we realize, especially

---

17 *Life Together*, 118–20.

after recounting our sins aloud, that we are not "entitled" to it. Karl Rahner sees the element of surprise in every authentic confession as a phenomenon grounded in the very nature of God:

> We would not understand God at all, if we were to think, as Heine cynically expressed it, that it is God's "métier" or job to forgive. Forgiveness is the greatest and most incomprehensible miracle of the love of God because in it God communicates Himself to a human being who in the seeming banality of everyday life has had the effrontery to say *No* to God.[18]

With each confession, we are astonished yet again by the bounty of divine grace.

As a group, clergy can also be prone to perfectionism, hard on others and even harder on themselves. The "repeat offender" in us constantly puts us to shame. Perhaps after years of practicing confession, however, we may find to our surprise that we can start loving and accepting ourselves, warts and all, for the simple reason that God has been doing it all along. We begin to participate in God's own forgiveness of us; there are no other grounds for "forgiving ourselves." Our pride has been worn down just a bit—not because of the recurrent humiliation of confessing, but because the sheer patience and generosity of God overwhelms us. Bishop Frank Griswold tells a story of himself about how his expectations of censure were upended in one unforgettable confession:

> Some years ago I prepared what I thought would be the confession of a lifetime. I spent a week-long retreat preparing for it. I decided that the time was right for a brilliant review of Frank Griswold's consummate sinfulness. I scoured and ruthlessly explored every nook and cranny. As I made my way to the encounter with

---

18 Karl Rahner, SJ, "Penance" in his *Meditations on the Sacraments*, trans. Salvator Attanasio (New York: Seabury Press, 1977), 52.

the priest who was to hear this outpouring, I thought
to myself, "I bet he's never heard a confession like this
before." That should have tipped me off to the fact that
something other than repentance was at work in me.

In any event, I entered into the priest's presence
and poured out my list of things. Then I waited to see
what would happen. I hoped for at least a gasp, but it
did not come. Instead, horror of horrors, he smiled.
And he said, "Frank, welcome to the human condition." That was an instance of "quick-ey'd love," to
borrow from George Herbert, palpably present. The
sacramental encounter with Christ on that occasion
was in the smile and words of my confessor. The rest
was irrelevant. I had been caught in a place of self-
deception, and his compassionate smile brought it
fully to light.[19]

For most of us, most of the time, "something other than repentance"
is at work in us even when we make our confessions. Disappointment in
ourselves, frustration at our lack of progress, shame at our backsliding,
panic or remorse over a serious sin, or the spiritual pride arising from
the admirable thoroughness of our self-examination to which this passage alludes are all possible contaminants to the purity of our confession. But what else could be expected from the likes of us? Even the
humiliation we feel from simply telling the truth about ourselves is an
evident symptom of pride. We bring it all to the mercy seat of Christ,
even those sins and flaws of which we are not yet aware. Our liturgies of penitence mention sins both "known and unknown" and those
"which I cannot now remember." Christ sweeps them all away. The role
of the confessor in this story is crucial, both in the words of absolution,
to be sure, and also in his bearing towards the penitent. When Frank

---

19 Frank T. Griswold, "Listening with the Ear of the Heart," *CrossCurrents* 49:1 (Spring 1999):
13–14.

Griswold was "caught in a place of self-deception" during his confession, he did not find this revelation one more item to add to his "consummate sinfulness." It was a liberation. The sweetness of his confessor's smile and his simple words conveyed the truth of his condition while mediating "the sacramental encounter with Christ." Griswold learned something about himself in that confession, but far more significantly, he learned something about Jesus' way with him.

Only this kind of regular exposure to sacramental confession can teach us how grace works through it. We are, of course, changed in the process, as we grow in wonder at the many ways Christ shows up in this sacrament. When the time comes for us to serve as confessors, then, we have ample grounds for confidence not in our own wealth of insight, but in the utter faithfulness of God. For giving counsel in confession does not depend on mastering a technique or storing up enough nuggets of wisdom to pose as an enlightened guru. Instead it is a matter of faith, of trusting that the Holy Spirit will provide the apt word at the right time, using our own humanity in the process. Naturally we will learn aspects of the art of hearing confessions from the good confessors who have ministered to us, just as we will recognize what to avoid from the bungling or insensitive confessors we may have encountered as well. The counseling given in confession is a form of preaching the gospel, personalized, and addressed briefly and in all simplicity to the one person present. Chapter four will deal with this topic of advice and counsel, but it is worth noting that our experience as penitents shapes our intuition about what sort of counsel rings true to our condition and what comes across as deadening moralism or pious cliché.

So far we have been considering why clergy need to make use of sacramental confession in order to be formed as able ministers of this rite. Besides gaining a measure of pastoral competence, however, there are still deeper reasons why clergy stand in special need of its grace. Pastoral ministry can often be lonely, and nothing makes us feel more isolated than the knowledge of our sinfulness. Even in the best circumstances, in which pastors feel supported and loved by the communities they serve, there is a necessary distance between priest and people. On top of all the material that we must hold in strict professional confidentiality, there is much we cannot disclose of our ruminations about the parish, school, or other community where we work. We should not aggravate this inevitable loneliness by being all alone in our sin.

The matter can be made worse by the powerful projections of holiness and wisdom that congregations often thrust upon their clergy. In some cases these idealizations can act as a hidden undertow, pulling us out of contact with our humanity and our need for God's forgiveness. When clergy identify with this "ideal" self, they become aloof, even when maintaining a certain heartiness in their demeanor. Yet a fundamental lack of compassion seeps out every now and then in indifference, outbursts of anger, or even verbal cruelty. In other cases, clergy may develop cynicism towards themselves and the people who look up to them—if only they knew! Some clergy react to being placed on a pedestal by abruptly jumping off and embarrassing their congregations by publicly rehearsing their failures, sins, doubts, unhappy personal relationships, or other struggles. Still others rip off the mask by drinking to excess at parish gatherings, using vulgar language, or finding some other ploy to convince their charges that they are "no saint." Now the tables have been turned, and the congregation has to worry about taking care of the priest.

This problem is rooted, not in the congregation's idealization of the priest, but in the priest's own failure to appreciate the positive role of projection in psychological and spiritual healing. Clergy are powerfully symbolic figures, even when they are not wearing vestments or other distinctive clothing. They are perceived as spiritual fathers and mothers, stand-ins for God. A more potent psychological brew can scarcely be imagined! Only clergy with professional psychological training might be able to direct these projections to a particular therapeutic end—and here again, such clergy would be working as therapists rather than as priests. The rest of us can simply sit lightly to these projections, realizing that they are not really about us, and let them do their work over time. If we mock them or try to undermine them, we may jeopardize a healing process, and seem to ridicule people and their highest aspirations. After all, this kind of idealization represents a notion of holiness that is the destiny of all the baptized. Given the right conditions and the operation of grace, these projections will gradually diminish, becoming interiorized and appropriated in authentic Christian maturity.

In the meantime, clergy need safe places where they can simply be human, although this does not mean lapsing into the regressive and self-indulgent behavior that is all too familiar at clergy gatherings. It is rather a matter of honoring and enlarging our humanity. Play and exercise, immersion in nature, and enjoyment of the arts can help us gain some perspective about our place in creation. Setting aside time to cultivate warm family bonds and friendships free of professional responsibilities is essential. But we will still need to deal with the gap between our public persona and the underside of what we know about ourselves. This disparity can create a stressful inner tension, even without the inevitable projections that get directed our way. It can even lead to depression, self-hatred, or despair. We can feel fraudulent in the exercise of our ministry as that old stereotype of the hypocritical priest comes uncomfortably close to home.

For this reason, no pastor should be without pastoring. We, too, are members of the body of Christ and just as reliant on priestly ministrations. As Hugh Wybrew writes about the spiritual requirements of clergy:

> Just as other Christians need help and guidance if they are to grow in prayer and Christian living, so priests and deacons need help themselves. They should each have a spiritual father or mother, with whom they can discuss regularly their relationship with God and with other people, and the practice of their ministry, its progress and problems. They should look for loving encouragement and gentle guidance—and when

necessary, firm correction. Ordination gives no protection from the temptations to which all Christians are
likely to give way, nor to those peculiar to the clergy
to which they not infrequently succumb. Those who
offer the ministry of reconciliation, absolving others
in the name of Christ, need themselves to receive it.[20]

The sacrament of reconciliation creates an absolutely safe zone in
which we can be free to be ourselves, sinners in need of Christ's compassionate mercy who can experience the joy of God's welcoming embrace
at our return. We discover anew our baptismal self-in-Christ. We are
beloved of God not because we are model priests or pastors, brilliant
preachers, or expert administrators. God loves us as we are in Christ; and
in Christ, we undergo the baptismal death to sin and rising to his new
life. The joy and thanksgiving involved in meeting Christ as our savior
then grounds the practice of our ministry. We can dare to be engaged in
this work because it is not ours, after all, but his-in-us. As a wise priest
once remarked, "Preaching is what comes after we're forgiven."[21] It holds
true not just for preaching, but for all ministerial life.

What Makes a Good Confessor?

The Exhortation in the earliest Book of Common Prayer (1549) advised
penitents to open their "sin and grief" to a "discreet and learned priest."
The revised version in the American Book of Common Prayer has a
"discreet and understanding" priest, but the quality of "understanding"
in this case means not only a compassionate grasp of human nature, but
theological and moral understanding—or learning—as well. These two
qualities of discretion and learned understanding are, as Cranmer first
recognized, essential for the fruitful administration of the rite. What do
they entail and how might we cultivate their growth within ourselves?

20 Hugh Wybrew, *Called to be Priests* (Oxford: SLG Press, 1989), 20.
21 Edward C. Coolidge, quoted in Julia Gatta, *The Nearness of God: Parish Ministry as Spiritual Practice* (New York: Morehouse, 2010), 85.

Discretion refers, among other things, to the capacity to exercise prudence and reserve in speech and behavior. We do not need to say or do everything that occurs to us; even our best insights and brightest ideas require the right circumstances to be properly expressed. In hearing confessions, our words to the penitent will have to be relatively brief and compressed, for this is not the time for lengthy discourse or extended conversation. Discretion may also require us to refrain from a line of questioning with the penitent that would be entirely suitable in a different context, such as a counseling session. Or we may find that we have to hold in check some advice that we think could benefit the penitent in other circumstances. We are instead to listen carefully to him and to whatever gospel word the Holy Spirit may prompt in us as we listen.

Another aspect of discretion involves a clear and unshakeable adherence to the seal of the confessional. The seal is absolute and admits of no exceptions whatsoever; the obligation it imposes does not expire even upon the death of the penitent. The rubrics to the various rites for private confession in Anglican and other churches impose this stringent discipline on all confessors. In this way the seal sets confession apart from other forms of professional confidentiality. In all sorts of communication with pastors, especially anything that is disclosed in counseling settings, a strict standard of professional confidentiality is required.

Yet at certain times our obligation to those who have communicated their secrets to us outside the parameters of sacramental confession is overridden by a higher moral obligation. For example, in most states clergy are officially identified as "mandated reporters" in cases of child abuse; they are legally bound to report any cases they learn of in the course of their counseling or in other situations. But the church's rule of the seal of confession insists that the secrecy surrounding disclosure made in the rite of sacramental reconciliation may not be broken for any reason whatever, including legal obligations imposed by the state. Certain countries and states legally protect the right of priests to refuse to speak of matters revealed to them in confession; others customarily refrain from putting the loyalty of priests to the discipline of the church to the test in the witness box. However, some states do not give any recognition to a priest's duty to keep the seal. If we are to exercise this ministry in these places, we must be prepared to run the risk of being held in contempt of court and undergoing a penalty for our silence.

Strict adherence to this rule is a basic condition for exercising the ministry of sacramental reconciliation in the church. If priests were free to decide when they might reveal the secrets of penitents, the essential security needed to make a full confession would be completely undermined. We might be able to imagine situations in which this strict adherence to the seal would prevent us from taking steps that might protect someone from danger or even death. This prospect can feel exceedingly burdensome and highly stressful, and might even discourage us from taking on the ministry of confession. But despite the exploitation of such scenarios by movies and TV, such occurrences are extremely rare and in most cases preventable. Sacraments, including that of reconciliation, should not be administered to those who are unprepared to receive them. Since nowadays confessions are rarely heard anonymously in a confessional box, priest and penitent are usually acquainted with one another. But if someone is unknown to us, a preliminary conversation is in order to ascertain her familiarity with and understanding of this sacrament. If we have any reason to doubt her motives or preparation, we should make sure before beginning the rite that the person seeking absolution understands that both contrition and the desire to make amends are required at the outset.

What if someone does disclose a crime in confession but has no desire or plan for restitution? Then we are obligated to bring him to the point where he understands the absolute necessity of reparation and restitution to people whom he has injured. This may mean accepting responsibility for the crime and going to the authorities, especially if there is any chance that an innocent party might otherwise fall under suspicion. In the hard case of someone who has confessed to child abuse, the confessor has to make it crystal clear that true repentance requires the penitent to act immediately to ensure that the child receive all necessary help and protection. Moreover, abusers must promise to stop the damaging conduct or, in the case of compulsive behavior, remove themselves from the situation and seek professional help. No confessor should absolve a penitent who does not agree to these obligations towards himself and those whom he had harmed. Thus absolution would only be given on the understanding that it will become void should the penitent fail to carry out these next steps. It is appalling to contemplate the possibility of refusing absolution to someone who has come to confession with defective motivation, and then have to keep silent about a case that we would certainly have reported had it been disclosed to us in a regular counseling session. Yet this is what the seal requires. In our Anglican situation, however, cases in which absolution has to be withheld are so rare that most priests will not encounter a single one in an entire lifetime of ministry.

The seal of confession covers more than verbal and written communication. The behavior and bearing of the confessor towards the penitent must remain unchanged, and may not be altered in any way that might seem to indict her or provoke misgivings. No action may be taken that could arouse suspicion. The priest must give communion, for example, to someone who comes forward to receive the sacrament even if absolution has been withheld. (The disciplinary rubrics and canons relating to the excommunication of public, notorious sinners still hold; however, priests must be certain that the knowledge they have of the situation can also be obtained outside of confession.) In the aftermath of confession, moreover, only the penitent may take the initiative to refer to matters disclosed in it; the priest is not free to bring them up, not even in a confidential meeting. However, in the course of hearing the confession, a priest could say something like, "If you would find it helpful to explore this matter in the future in further counseling, feel free to raise the subject. Any further discussion we have will be under the same conditions of absolute secrecy that now prevail in this sacramental confession." The penitent, then, must be the one to raise the matter in subsequent discussion, and any counseling that might ensue would take place as an extension of the counsel given in confession. The seal of confession would continue to apply to it. Finally, although not technically a breach of this seal, it is a breach of pastoral discretion to mention who comes to us for confession and who does not. Since it is standard practice in counseling to protect the identity of clients, a similar standard certainly applies to the even more sensitive ministry of sacramental confession. Penitents, of course, are free to offer this information to others, but pastors should avoid such revelations.

In order to hear confessions responsibly, a pastor must be sufficiently equipped in moral theology to guide penitents who may be confused about their moral choices and actions. This is why the tradition upholds the value of making one's confession to a "learned" or "understanding" priest. This is because some may confess behavior that is in fact morally neutral, or blame themselves for unavoidable setbacks or calamities. Others, whose consciences are insufficiently formed, may propose a line of action that has no theological backing and amounts to an evasion of responsibility. In either case the confessor will have to intervene, sometimes gently, sometimes firmly, by offering counsel, teaching, or direction.

In still other instances, the confessor will need enough knowledge, sensitivity, and self-restraint to deal with complex issues that straddle moral boundaries. In some areas of life prayerful and faithful reflection has given rise to differing moral positions within the household of faith. In these situations, we have to be prepared to honor the primacy of personal conscience and respect the conclusions drawn by those whose consciences work differently from our own. Our grasp of moral theology needs to be sufficiently deep and broad to allow us to recognize when a moral choice has significant responsible backing in the church, even when that choice goes against our own considered opinion of the matter. Casuistry is a living art—it is the careful and generous discernment of morally tangled situations. A dedicated pacifist, for example, might have difficulties with hearing the confession of a soldier returning from war. Aware of the long tradition of both pacifist and just war theories in the church, however, she would need to suspend her own deeply held convictions to hear the soldier's confession on his own terms.

The current debate about homosexual ethics offers another example of the way confessors must be prepared to work sympathetically with those who may differ from them. Up until about forty years ago, the moral consensus of the church denied the legitimacy of sexual unions between persons of the same sex and claimed that homosexuality brought with it a vocation to permanent celibacy. However, there is now substantial and serious support for the position that gay and lesbian Christians are acting in good faith when they enter committed, life-long partnerships that are sexually consummated. Of course, Christian moral theology still excludes promiscuity and serial monogamy as incompatible with the enduring, sacrificial love exemplified by Christ. Because the debate on homosexuality is often heated and bitter, it is all the more necessary for confessors to exercise sensitive discretion in this area. Accordingly, a confessor who personally endorsed the traditional teaching would need to refrain from attempting to overthrow the conscience of a penitent who had arrived at the alternative position prayerfully and conscientiously.

Another common example comes from the field of reproductive ethics. A confessor may believe that abortion is the lesser of two evils when certain conditions prevail. She may then hear the confession of a woman who expresses shame and guilt for an abortion under circumstances that she herself regards as justifiable. This is not a case of scrupulosity, but a different figuring of the moral calculus. How very careful she must be not to impose the operations of her own conscience upon the penitent, who may have genuinely come to believe that she was called by God to bear the child. Her sense of guilt and desire for forgiveness has weighty support from the church's tradition. In cases such as these the confessor must beware of contradicting beliefs arising from the penitent's own informed conscience.

Another way to exercise discretion in hearing confessions is by refraining to offer premature consolation. Sensitive people are discomforted by seeing others in pain, and many clergy are naturally disposed to offer sympathy and reassurance to those in distress. But pastors who have confronted their own shadowy self in silent prayer, self-examination, sacramental confession, or therapy know that some forms of inner turmoil cannot be sidestepped on the road to maturity and freedom. Sometimes we have to respect people enough to allow them to undergo their own particular anguish. Without promoting a morbid cult of suffering, we can nonetheless recognize that the "death to sin" will not be easy: participation in the cross of Christ will hurt. Confessors who have been through this crucible will not deny it to others. A confessor who can remain tranquil amid tears and emotional storms can inspire trust in God, the rock of our salvation. This is not stoicism, but rather a way of embodying the hope that the penitent will, by the grace of God, win through to resurrection joy. So we do nothing to block the pain or undermine the process by which the paschal mystery is unfolding in a particular life.

Underlying the twin attributes of discretion and understanding must be a prayerful openness to God. One listens to a confession with a peaceful—not tense—attentiveness to God present in the room. Since it is the Holy Spirit who convicts us of our sins, we know that this Spirit has been at work in the penitent, stirring her to contrition and animating her desire for divine forgiveness. As confessors we come alongside our penitents, sharing in their prayer and interceding for them, perhaps silently, before the throne of divine grace. Archbishop Michael Ramsey spoke of priestly intercession as being called "near to Jesus and with Jesus, *to be with God with the people on our heart.*"[22] If we can allow ourselves to be centered in Christ as we hear confessions,

---

22 Michael Ramsey, *The Christian Priest Today* (London: SPCK, 1972), 14.

the sense of divine presence can be almost palpable: we are with God with this person on our heart. There is grace for us in this sacrament as there is grace for the penitent. The Holy Spirit is directing this confession, and Christ is present in us as his representative. This quality of God-centeredness is accompanied by a sense of authority to act on God's behalf, and an awareness of the power and seriousness of the sacramental act. We are humbled by the grace of ordination that has allowed us to be vessels of Christ's own ministry to repentant sinners.

Prayerful openness to God prompts us to speak the word of God directly and spontaneously. The counsel given in confession is a form of preaching the gospel to the penitent—telling him how Christ is with him, how God regards him, and how he is being invited to exercise faith, hope, and love in response to God's forgiveness and compassion. That is why confession is not the setting for reassuring conversation, friendly advice, or acting as a sounding board. We are speaking about God, and about how God is acting at this moment to give new life in Christ: the baptismal grace of participation in Jesus' death and resurrection is being renewed. A confessor should be at ease in praying aloud with the penitent; in this sacramental setting, simple straightforward words often have terrific resonance and power. The subsequent absolution and laying-on-of-hands can be felt by the penitent to be momentous and awesome.

How Hearing Confessions Changes Us

Administering any of the sacraments inevitably affects those who administer them. If we offer the sacraments in a rote or blasé manner, sacramental ministry will contribute to the coarsening of our own hearts. Over time, we will come to treat sacred things, occasions, and people with indifference or irreverence, effectively creating a wall between ourselves and the interventions of grace. But if we administer the sacraments with prayer and careful spiritual preparation, with loving attention to the Christ at work in them, we can experience wave upon wave of divine grace as we minister to others. Sacramental ministry gives us a particular vantage point from which to view God's overwhelming generosity and Christ's self-giving love. We stand at that intersection between God and the people, sensing powerful currents of grace in action. Karl Rahner once described the life of the priest as a calling that allows us "to dwell completely in the explicit nearness of God." Each act of ministry, each sacrament, incarnates God's nearness in a different way. How does this happen in the course of hearing confessions?

Because confessions differ from one another, the particular graces for penitent and confessor will vary, too. We are bound to hear the confessions of people who differ widely from us in age, temperament, education, social class, family situation, and spiritual formation. This variety stretches and humbles us. We may feel intimidated by hearing the confessions of people who are highly educated, or very wealthy, or more spiritually mature than ourselves. These are occasions when we remember that we do not exercise this ministry on the basis of our own merits but on the grace of our ordination, which charged us to minister to everyone in an even-handed way. Young and old, rich and poor, strong and weak: all need Christ and his ministry. The Spirit is inviting us in these situations to move past our own self-regard to trust in God. From time to time we will also be called to exercise patience towards those whose confessions are digressive and rambling.

Some confessions will present disturbing material to our imaginations. We may hear about atrocious evil or sickeningly twisted behavior. If we are shocked or distressed, we must not show it in any way, but remain outwardly calm and unruffled. Charity requires such an exercise in self-control, and besides, something more significant is transpiring here than our natural human reactions. The penitent is in the process of being freed from these sins, perhaps laboriously released bit by bit. We listen to confessions with the ears of Christ, seated in his place, with renewed awe at the magnitude of love that has borne all these sins. Our prayer during and after painful, exhausting confessions will include strong intercession for the penitent and also for ourselves.

Our faith in the power of God to renew lives through the cross and resurrection might be challenged—but also strengthened—after such confessions. Through them we have witnessed the grace of conversion operating at a deep level, and we have seen at first hand the desire of God "to deliver their soul from death" those who "hope in his steadfast love" (Psalm 33:19, 18).

The vulnerability of the penitent in confession is apparent, but there is a corresponding vulnerability entailed in hearing confessions, too. While it is true that every pastoral encounter, every pastoral activity (even a committee meeting), may deliver some wound or fresh burden, hearing confessions requires an exceptional openness to whatever sin or grace may present itself at the time. We approach this sacrament with no agenda except to mediate the forgiveness of Christ, and we cannot know ahead of time the precise shape that will take, aside from the words of absolution. We come as a *tabula rasa*, allowing ourselves to be moved, pained, saddened, or edified. It is impossible to know in advance what will happen, not even with those whose confessions we regularly receive. In fact, the dynamic of the sacrament requires a cultivated, intentional, unguarded availability to both the penitent and to God throughout the rite. Such a radical throwing open of the doors of our heart is good for our souls.

Hearing confessions can also deepen our charity. "If anyone is detected in a transgression," counsels St. Paul, "you who have received the Spirit should restore such a one in a spirit of gentleness. . . . Bear one another's burdens, and in this way you will fulfill the law of Christ" (Galatians 6:1–2). What is the ministry of sacramental confession except such a bearing of another's burdens, the shouldering of a fellow sinner's load until all is consigned to the mercy of Christ? In confession we share the heaviness of those weighed down with serious sin, the struggles of committed Christians endeavoring to live more faithfully but still hampered by innumerable failings, and all those falling in between. We are privy to the hidden pain of those who appear successful in the world and happy in their personal relationships. The ocean of sin, sadness, and suffering that we encounter in confession cannot help but enlarge our compassion, literally, our capacity for "suffering with" others. Some priests claim that their attitude towards those who come to them for confession does not change after hearing their confessions, but this is unlikely. These pastors no doubt wish to reassure their penitents or their congregations that they do not disdain anyone for what has been confessed, and that is probably true. But we are changed from within—in most cases, we are bound to love people more when we have been privileged to stand with them in such an exposed place before God.

For both confessors and penitents, sacramental reconciliation is above all a meeting with the Risen Lord. Christ imparts his victory over sin in an atmosphere that is finally one of joy and peace, no matter how many tears have been shed during the course of a confession. All the human misery and guilt we have encountered is held and then blotted out by the still larger abyss of divine love, the power of God to recreate the world. Because all sacraments flow from the resurrection and point towards the restoration of all things in Christ, we experience them as profoundly hopeful and renewing. So our faith and hope, along with our charity, is increased by the grace of God as we participate in these sacramental actions.

Hearing confessions, like pastoral ministry generally, can also offer us some perspective on our own spiritual lives. It is not that we compare ourselves to others, but that we are allowed to see at close range the universal need for grace revealed in one particular life after another. Consequently our own difficulties might no longer loom so large; and even if they do, we may have gained a more developed sense of how they bind us to the suffering of others like unseen connective tissue. And because we have repeatedly observed the generosity of God towards others, we grow in confidence that God's compassionate care and redemptive love includes us, too.

We cannot bring a calm, centered prayerfulness to hearing confessions if we do not allocate significant time for silence with God at other regular intervals. Perhaps one grace of hearing confessions is simply that it sharpens what is true of all ministry, both lay and ordained: we cannot do it without sustained prayer. We know this, and we have made ordination promises to be faithful to the practice of prayer and other spiritual disciplines. Yet many of us have allowed the intimacy with God for which we yearn to get edged out of our lives. We have many good excuses, and there is always more work to be done. But hearing confessions without being grounded in a steady life of prayer courts disaster. The pastoral responsibility to "do no harm," if nothing else, must awaken our conscience here. Back in 1931, a priest called G.W. Hockley opened an address to a convention of clergy in London by putting the matter squarely:

> The twenty-sixth of the "Articles of Religion" reminds us that "the unworthiness of the Minister hinders not the effect of the Sacrament." That is a sound and comforting doctrine. But in any case it is one more profitably pondered by the laity than the clergy. And in the case of the Sacrament of Penance, the Holy Spirit makes very direct use of the individual character and personality of the priest.[23]

The point is not that we should be scared away from the ministry of reconciliation because of an exaggerated sense of unworthiness or deficiency. That excuse could just be an evasion of responsibility. We may not be blessed with extraordinary gifts of insight or intuition, but every Christian is called to holiness. We grow into ever greater union with Christ through all the familiar yet marvelous ways that have come down to us through the church: by frequent participation in the eucharist and the other sacraments, prayerful study of the scriptures, disciplines like the daily office, simple conversational prayer, various forms of meditation, and loving silent attention to the presence of God. These practices

23 G.W. Hockley, "The Priest as Confessor" in *The Priest in the Confessional*, ed. J.F. Briscoe (London: Faith Press, 1931), 48.

form the mind of Christ in us, a habit of mind in which we begin to see people, events, and situations as Christ does. The importance of this disposition for pastors and confessors cannot be exaggerated.

Jesus calls his disciples friends and not just servants (John 15:15). The invitation is for us, too. Friendship with Christ gives him a real foothold in our lives, a space in which to exercise his risen ministry through us. The ordinary spiritual disciplines of the church will make us more able ministers of Christ because they shape us to his-life-in-us. We can speak confidently of God's ways because we know them for ourselves.

CHAPTER THREE

Preparing for Confession and Celebrating the Rite

The prospect of making a first confession can feel intimidating. Helping people prepare for their first experience of sacramental confession therefore calls for much more than a few quick tips. Very few people have been shown how to examine their consciences or sift through their behavior and motives to discern what calls for the forgiveness of God. We have to recognize that if, immediately after a Sunday eucharist, we were to ask the members of our congregations to write down the specific sins for which they had received absolution during the service, most of them would find it impossible. Usually we will need to devote a substantial pastoral conversation to help them explore the art of self-examination. We need to give people an approach, even a plan, that makes the task of naming their sins less daunting than it may at first seem to the inexperienced.

A pastor needs to devote prayer and thoughtfulness to this

preparatory coaching. Helping someone prepare for confession is actually a remarkable privilege because what we are about is close to the very heart of the gospel. This is serious work that draws on some of the most intimate spiritual gifts that a priest cultivates. And it is an opportunity to be aware with gratitude that we are truly acting as agents of the Holy Spirit. There is a lot at stake in the sensitivity we display as we help people bring to awareness the sins that God is yearning to forgive. In the work of preparation we have the opportunity to express God's tenderness, understanding, and compassion in advance of the actual celebration of the rite.

Making a Life Confession

In a few cases, someone will come to us with one main sin that she feels the need to confess, and it is entirely legitimate for that to be virtually the sole focus of a sacramental confession. So we verify with the penitent that she has genuinely experienced God's forgiveness for other sins. We assure her that the rite of reconciliation is available as a remedy addressing an exception, where personal prayer and the eucharist have not proved adequate in bringing about a sense of God's forgiveness in the case of a particular behavior or failure. However, if we sense there is no immediate urgency in the desire to come to the rite of reconciliation, and are careful not to exert pressure, we would be wise to explore an alternative approach to this confession of a single sin. So we may ask whether she would like to use this opportunity to make a confession that also includes the other sins committed up to this point, even though she has already felt forgiven for them—in other words, a life confession.

We might gently raise this possibility on the grounds that making a life confession can bring a rich sense of completeness, making the rite of reconciliation a genuine milestone in the spiritual journey, bringing with it a sense of a completely fresh start. Going further, we can share with the penitent the experience of those who have examined their conscience in this comprehensive and thorough way, and discovered that it enabled the Holy Spirit to bring some aspect of their brokenness to light that they had overlooked. Including these sins of which we become newly aware through self-examination broadens the effect of absolution and deepens the experience of healing.

If the penitent decides to take this opportunity to prepare a first confession that covers the sins of a lifetime, then we can go on to offer some guidelines for the process of self-examination. Martin L. Smith's *Reconciliation: Preparing for Confession in the Episcopal Church* offers a full range of guidelines, and we might recommend or lend this book for use in preparation. It is also helpful for penitents to take notes during this exploratory conversation so they can remember the main points.

One of the first questions likely to occur is: how long does it take to prepare for a life confession? It is a good question, because self-examination is a process that works in harmony with the rhythms of our deeper levels of consciousness. It cannot be forced. On the other hand, there is no need for it to be protracted over months, as if that could ensure exhaustive results. We just need to give God enough time to stir our memories and to walk lovingly with us on pathways through our heart that tend to be badly lit. A commonsense answer to the question might be along these lines: "It is normal to find that we need three to six weeks. That gives time for our conscience to open up and usually culminates in an intuitive sense of completeness, a feeling that the work has been done, even though we know that there are bound to be sins we have forgotten."

Another question that a penitent may find himself struggling with is: "Is this self-examination process going to suck me into a state of anxious introspection that drags on and on? Will I find myself getting depressed, constantly raking over my failings, and brooding over my shortcomings?" This kind of apprehensiveness and other misgivings are best addressed by talking with the penitent about the importance of gently handing over the process to the indwelling Spirit of God. The Spirit dwells in our hearts and is at work within us as a nurse and confidante, not as an inquisitor. God uses self-examination not to hurt us, but to help us "find where it hurts" so that wounds can be dressed and healed. It is helpful to recommend praying with Psalm 139, and to point to various passages of Scripture that witness to this inner work of guidance and support by the Spirit.

Taking the First Steps

We can reassure someone seeking confession for the first time that self-examination works best in short sessions of reflection and prayer, usually a few days apart. This is perfectly manageable and allows us to get on with our normal routines. Nothing is to be gained from trying to probe our consciences for hours on end. If we rely on short focused periods of reflection, not more than half an hour at a time, we can then let the unconscious continue to work subliminally for a while before we take up the thread again.

Here are some of the initial "best practices" clergy can recommend:.

- Take notes that you can eventually bring with you to the confession. Don't use a journal, laptop computer, or any kind of electronic device that could preserve them after the confession. Keep them private in a secure place.

- Divide your life up into five or six distinct periods that you can recall in turn. These could be as simple as: childhood, adolescence, young adulthood, and so on. Or there could be other divisions that reflect your particular life experience: the years of your first marriage, the time since you came out, the period of your military service, and your retirement.

- Use these periods as headings on separate pages. Then begin by asking God to keep you company and support you as you bring back into awareness actions that were

unloving and wrong, and ways in which, out of mistrust
and fear, you failed to act.

Those who are coming to confession because a particular event
is weighing on their conscience will usually begin by focusing on the
period of their life during which it took place. Otherwise it does not
matter in what order penitents look at the various phases of their lives.
Our advice may continue along these lines:

"As you focus on each phase of your life in turn, think of your
life as a whole. Don't be in too much of a hurry to focus on negative
things—include the good things, too. This is important because as
we look back we may discover that there were indeed many gifts we
experienced which we took for granted at the time. Sin may have been
present in our lives simply as ingratitude. Furthermore, don't censor
your thoughts—if you remember something that seems quite trivial
from an adult point of view, don't dismiss it if you distinctly remember
sensing it was wrong. For example, it is quite common to experience
guilt and shame over something like an incident of cruelty to an animal
when we were children. It is never too late to experience God's forgiveness for something that happened when our sense of moral responsibility was still in its earliest days.

"As you spend time recalling your life in its distinct phases, you are
likely to be drawn back into a sense of the distinct challenges you were
contending with at that particular stage of your growth. For example,
as adolescents most of us are struggling with issues of independence,
identity, and sexual maturation, and some of our failings from that
period were almost unavoidable. Yet by putting them into straightforward words for confession we can let God's grace heal some of the
wounds we received and inflicted at the time. As we review our lives in
their distinct phases, we are likely to find ourselves growing in compassion towards ourselves, a sure sign of God's loving Spirit at work.

"After you have revisited each period of your life, and noted down
the sins that have come to light, you are likely to reach a point where

you don't seem able to add anything more. This is the time for a second phase of self-examination where we use the resources of Scripture, and other exercises of reflection, to open ourselves to fresh insights."

Scripture as the Basis of Self-Examination

When it comes to recommending specific passages of Scripture, it is helpful to have ready a one-page handout listing some of the most useful ones. Not all of your parishioners will have sufficient knowledge of the Bible to be able to find them for themselves, and it is easy to embarrass a penitent inadvertently who might be sensitive about a lack of familiarity with the Bible. A basic of list of Scripture passages is likely to include the following:

- 1 Corinthians 13: Love

    Let each of St. Paul's statements about the way love operates shed light on your own unloving tendencies. For example, "Love is not resentful." What part has resentment played in your life? Do you nurse grudges? Whom won't you forgive? Has someone else's success made you wish they had failed?

- Exodus 20: The Ten Commandments

    Take each commandment in turn, and let it set off a train of thought. For example, "You shall not bear false witness against your neighbor" might set you thinking about times in which you have spread rumors and gossip, or deliberately damaged someone's reputation.

- Mark 12:28–31: Jesus' Summary of the Law

    Think about the centrality of God in your life as you ponder Jesus' reminder about the invitation to "love God with your all your heart, and with all your soul, and with all your mind, and with all your strength." This first and great commandment urges us to see that God is present in all aspects of our lives.

Are there areas of your life that you tend to treat as your own business, and so forget God's presence and claims on your love? Then there is the commandment to love your neighbor as yourself. Are there any people whom you have disqualified from being truly your neighbor? Have you withheld love, respect, and help where it was needed, turning away from a fellow human being? As for loving ourselves, remember that any hatred and disrespect towards ourselves goes against God's love and tenderness for us, and is likely to diminish our ability to honor and support others.

- Matthew 5, 6: The Sermon on the Mount

  Read a few verses at a time and use your imagination to see patterns in your own behavior that correspond to Jesus' searching analysis. For example, his question, "Why do you see the speck in your neighbor's eye, but do not notice the log in your own eye?" might trigger memories of ways in which you have judged others harshly, especially criticizing them for faults that you yourself are prone to.

- Galatians 5:22–26: The Fruits of the Spirit

  Think of the signs of spiritual freedom and generosity that result from trust in the indwelling Spirit of love: love, joy, peace, patience, kindness, generosity, faithfulness, gentleness, and self-control. Ponder ways in which you have displayed the opposite characteristics.

The Seven Deadly Sins and Other Approaches to Self-Examination

An additional aid to reflection is the traditional list of sinful traits known as the seven deadly sins: pride, greed, anger, lust, envy, gluttony, sloth. You may want to give the penitent this list, and then offer some brief suggestions about how it can throw light on patterns of behavior in our lives.

- Pride

  Reflect on how you insist on your own way, expecting others to regard you as superior to them. Notice times when you have been reluctant to admit mistakes or things you don't know, and when you have resisted apologizing or have refused to seek help. Do you acknowledge your need of others and your indebtedness to them? Have you actively sought the grace of humility? Consider, too, the phenomenon of inverted pride. Sometimes we think of ourselves as unique or special in a negative way, as exceptionally inadequate, weak, or unqualified to make any contribution.

- Greed

  Think of ways in which you feel the need to gratify acquisitive impulses, especially as a willing participant in the consumerism of our society. Do you use people and things to satisfy inner cravings? Have you actively sought the grace of contentment?

- Envy

  Think of ways in which you are caught up in comparing your life with those of others. Have you resented others' success? Have you nursed disappointment and lack of respect for your own life, your own path and gifts? Have you actively sought to cultivate gratitude?

- Anger

  Think of ways in which you have resorted to emotional or even physical violence against others. Have you been abusive and bullying? Or have you fumed and withdrawn from others and damaged relationships by refusing to deal with conflict in an open, honest way? Have you withheld forgiveness from anyone who has sought it? Have you actively sought God's help to be someone who seeks peace and reconciliation?

• Lust

Think of ways in which you have used others, especially for sexual gratification, or sought sexual stimulus outside the context of a committed and loving relationship. Can you see in your life any tendency to deceive yourself in the ways you have acted sexually, perhaps by making more of a relationship than is really there to justify sexual intimacy?

• Gluttony

Are you dependent on overeating, drinking heavily, or using drugs to satisfy cravings or cover up difficult emotions? Have you sought help to bring eating and drinking within the bounds of health? Do you hold yourself accountable for cultivating health as a gift of God?

• Sloth

Think about ways in which you are indolent, avoiding the cost of discipline and effort to meet the demands of life and Christian discipleship. Do you procrastinate? Do you seek the recreative sabbath rest that God wants us to enjoy? Think of other terms for sloth, such as apathy and indifference. Do they suggest ways in which you avoid acting and taking responsibility in your life? Can you remember using excuses like "There's no point in even trying"?

A further technique for self-examination is to consider the various roles we play in our lives, and take them in turn, asking God to help us recognize any failings in each area. We can reflect on our lives as workers, as spouses, as parents, as sons and daughters, as members of the church, as citizens, and as denizens of this fragile planet for whose health we are responsible.

A final recommendation will be to make sure that when the period of self-examination has come to an end, the penitent goes over the notes to remove any references to other people by name. We can also suggest a final editing to remove unnecessary details. A confession is not a life history, and we need only include the minimum information that gives the context for our sins.

When we have offered our guidance and answered any questions the penitent may have, we can conclude with a simple extemporaneous prayer of blessing and encouragement as she begins her own work of preparation. Eventually we will set an appointment time for the rite.

Physical Settings for the Rite of Reconciliation

As pastors we are responsible for choosing the appropriate setting for administering the rite of reconciliation. There is a range of possibilities that it is good to discuss beforehand as part of the penitent's preparation. We can hear confessions in a church, in a room in our church buildings that has been set aside exclusively for this and other private pastoral conversations, or in a neutral setting such as our office or study. Each setting has its merits and drawbacks. Before examining these in turn, we can recognize there are bound to be occasional exceptions. We may be called on to hear a confession in a hospital room, in the home of someone confined by illness or disability, on a bench by a quiet lakeside during a retreat. As pastors we should be prepared for these varied circumstances, especially by committing the essential prayers to memory, and being vigilant about ensuring sufficient privacy for the rite wherever it takes place.

Hearing confessions in church, in the same sacred space where we celebrate baptisms and the eucharist, makes obvious theological sense. The creed affirms "one baptism for the forgiveness of sins" and to make a confession close to the font helps us remember that the costliness of confession and the joy of absolution are ways we experience the baptismal pattern of death and resurrection, of being born again as beloved children of God. Making a confession near the altar connects receiving forgiveness in confession with our experience of Holy Communion Sunday by Sunday: "This is my blood which is shed for you and for many for the forgiveness of sins." Administering the rite of reconciliation in church helps set it apart from other pastoral conversations and encounters; we are affirming that this is a liturgy of the church, a sacramental rite. Only two are gathered in the name of Christ, but he is in the midst of them, and together they make up a gathering of the church for worship.

If we are going to use the church for administering this rite, we need to be sure that our particular church building will in fact serve the purpose, with the chief criterion being our ability to guarantee confidentiality. Whatever the size of the church, it has to provide a sufficient buffer zone of privacy that eliminates the possibility that a third party might overhear either the penitent or the minister, or be close enough to observe their body language. And we need to be able to set aside the place for the rite in such a way that the penitent will feel at ease, and there will be nothing that causes strain or distraction as the rite unfolds. It is pastorally inept simply to turn up in church and seem vague about where to settle down. In the Anglican pastoral tradition, a typical arrangement is to have a chair for the priest with its back to a wall, and next to it, facing the wall, a prayer desk and kneeler for the penitent. In some places this is best set up in a quiet corner or aisle, perhaps near the font. In others, the preferable setting is a side chapel customarily used for prayer and smaller weekday celebrations of the eucharist. Where this is not practical, another arrangement is to place a chair for the priest inside the altar rail, facing inwards. The penitent can then kneel at the altar rail and be supported by it. Those who kneel for any length of time usually need something to lean on. We must recognize that many people will find kneeling physically impossible. In that case we must provide a chair for the penitent as well as the priest, and it is best to place them opposite each other at a slight angle to avoid an impression of confrontation.

A small number of our churches in the Anglo-Catholic tradition are furnished with confessionals, closet-like boxes fitted with an internal partition separating the penitent from the confessor. We can assume that these churches have a well-established practice of offering the rite, and parishioners may have come to appreciate the virtual anonymity confessionals provide. However, priests in these parishes should provide alternative settings and explain their respective merits whenever they are helping people prepare for confession. Confessionals may have negative associations for some people who are familiar with them only from melodramatic scenes in movies. Some may be susceptible to claustrophobia. It is important, moreover, to be frank about some of the disadvantages of confessionals. For example, they make the laying on of hands at the absolution impossible, a ritual that is now highly valued in modern pastoral practice.

In churches that are not normally open to people just dropping in, it is relatively easy to ensure sufficient privacy for the celebration of the rite. But steps may still have to be taken to prevent interruptions. In the middle of hearing a confession, we don't want suddenly to have to break off because members of the youth group have unexpectedly burst in to drop off some chairs they borrowed, or because the organist decided spontaneously to get in some practice. A simple temporary sign to hang on the door may be needed: "The church is in use for prayer just now: please come back in half an hour." In churches that are wide open to the public, the area set aside for confession must be far enough away from any area that a casual visitor might wander into, and it may also need to be protected by some kind of sign. Where there is a parish receptionist, it is wise to establish ahead of time that the church is reserved at this time.

Even when the actual rite of reconciliation takes place elsewhere in the parish facility, the church itself may have a part to play. For example, we may want to recommend that the penitent spend a short time after confession giving thanks in prayer, so we ought to ensure in advance that the church will be already open and appropriately lit. Then the penitent can go there straight away and find the space inviting and ready. Obviously, we won't make this recommendation if our church is unheated in winter except for Sunday services.

In practice, the church may not be the best pastoral setting for adults making a first confession that covers their whole life. Since these confessions may take well over forty-five minutes to unfold, a church setting may feel too exposed for this protracted experience and not conducive to the pastoral dialogue and counsel that a life confession may especially call for.

A second option that has been adopted in some churches with space available is to set aside a small room exclusively for one-to-one pastoral meetings. It need be furnished only with two simple chairs, a low table with a Bible, prayer books, a box of tissues, and an icon or crucifix on the wall that helps set the scene of holy encounter. Many Roman Catholic churches have set aside rooms like this, accessible from within the church or close to it in order to provide a more personal setting for celebrating the rite of reconciliation. Such a room ought not to feel closed in, inducing claustrophobia. It is good to have some natural light coming in, and the use of translucent curtains or lightly frosted glass can ensure that others cannot peer in on those celebrating the rite. Penitents should never see a face in the window!

The third option is to use our study or office. In this case we need to take very deliberate steps to make this setting congruent with the spirit of the sacramental rite, especially ensuring strict privacy by closing windows and connecting doors. In recent years there has been a movement to require that clergy offices have a small window in the door. This is supposed to lower the risk of clergy misconduct by making sure that a third party could potentially monitor what is occurring behind closed doors. Pastors whose offices have this kind of door still need to make sure that no one is going to observe a penitent directly in the act of making a confession. The pastor must turn off the telephone connections before the penitent arrives, and prevent interruptions by discreetly informing receptionists and, when necessary, mounting temporary signs on the door. If the office is spacious, a corner may be set up with a chair and a kneeler and prayer desk for those who may prefer to use this traditional posture. Otherwise, the rite will be celebrated with both priest and penitent sitting for most of the time. The seating is something to consider carefully, because sofas that have us sink into deep cushions and upholstery do not help us feel prayerful and centered. The priest is wise to avoid having two chairs directly facing each other; we are not inviting penitents to focus on us, nor should they feel confronted by us. Finally, in our physical preparations we should have ready at hand a Bible, two prayer books open at the rite of reconciliation, and a box of tissues in case the penitent weeps. When preparing to hear confessions in a study or office, there is no need for the priest to change into a cassock or vestments, but it is appropriate to have a stole available to put on over our ordinary clothes, as a visible sign that this is a sacramental rite.

Preparing to Celebrate the Rite

It is best for pastors to wear their usual clerical attire to hear confessions, since they are exercising priestly office. As we mentioned above, a stole should be worn throughout the rite. Putting the stole on just before the rite begins, and taking it off afterwards, is a very clear sign marking the boundaries of the confession, boundaries that protect the zone of absolute confidentiality. When the confession is heard in the church itself, it is normal and fitting to wear a cassock and surplice.

Just before the penitent is due to arrive, the pastor prepares briefly with prayer, asking for guidance and blessing. When he arrives, we should welcome him in a straightforward, natural way—a hushed, serious tone or hearty cheerfulness might both strike a false note. When both are settled, the pastor should clarify the liturgical choices available. If, as in the Book of Common Prayer of the Episcopal Church, there are alternative forms for the rite, we may invite the penitent to make a choice between the two, and unless this has already been explained in a previous conversation, it may be helpful to characterize the difference very briefly: "The first form of the rite is the simpler version, and the second form has prayers that use richer imagery for expressing our penitence for sin. Which one do you think you might prefer?"

Secondly, we can explain that some people prefer to remain sitting for the entire rite, except for the prayer of absolution itself at the end, when it is usual to kneel. Others may choose to kneel also for the prayer during which they actually confess their sins out loud, while some may want to kneel throughout the rite. We can then have a brief conversation that helps him choose what posture he wants to use. When we have a sense of his preferences, simple cues during the rite will help him change his posture, such as, "Now that you have confessed yours sins, I am ready to give you some brief words of counsel, so you can be seated again." After this preliminary conversation about posture and liturgical options, the priest will usually put on the priestly stole to signal the transition to the liturgy itself.

Using the Rite in the Context of Pastoral Conversations

From time to time cases will arise where the need or desire for sacramental confession emerges unforeseen during a pastoral conversation. For example, perhaps someone has made an appointment with a priest to talk over a problem or issue and to seek support, clarification, and advice. Confession was not on the agenda at all, but during the conversation she becomes aware that a particular behavior, current or past, calls for God's forgiveness. She now perceives it as sinful even though she may not have realized that before. At this point the priest has the option of proposing the use of the rite there and then, so that she may experience God's forgiveness and enact the choice to repent and make a fresh beginning without delay.

There is a risk that a pastor might proceed too casually and declare, "Well, you have really been making your confession informally during our counseling session, so why don't I give you absolution right away, and then you are good to go?" The danger is that no differentiation has been made between the actual behaviors that are sinful and other experiences and feelings that were expressed during the counseling session. The person seeking resolution may be left with the impression that most of the experiences she shared called for absolution. Then she may become confused about where lines of confidentiality, if any, are supposed to be drawn, given that the discussion about the particular sins was mixed up with all sorts of other personal matters that would not ordinarily fall under the seal of the confessional.

So if the pastor chooses to bring the rite of reconciliation into play in the context of counseling, it is wise to bring its sacramental nature into focus, so that it is not liable to lose its force in vague informality. Therefore it would be effective to say something like this:

> Let's take a moment to realize that we give God joy whenever we seek his forgiveness and turn towards him to give us a new beginning. Remember how Jesus spoke of there being "joy in heaven" whenever a sinner repents. In our conversation you have become aware of a need for his forgiveness, and the church has a special sacramental rite that we can use at times like this. We can confess our sins confidentially to a priest and receive absolution, a direct and personal assurance of God's forgiveness. Would you like us to celebrate that rite here and now so that you can experience that grace of forgiveness without delay?

Then the priest can spend a few moments going through the text of the rite and briefly explaining its meaning. All that is then needed is a simple cue recognizing that the penitent may already have confessed the sin in detail during the pastoral conversation: "Because we have already talked through the sins for which you are now seeking God's forgiveness, all you need do in the prayer of confession is to name the sins briefly and directly in your own words." Even though we may have already given ample counsel about these matters, at the conclusion of the confession we can still direct the penitent's attention toward the work of God's grace in her.

The Celebration of the Rite

How to begin the rite itself? It is often desirable to begin with a brief, extemporaneous prayer. It should call to mind the presence of Christ where two are gathered in his name, praise him for the gift of forgiveness that comes from his death for us, and give thanks that the Holy Spirit has guided the penitent to come to this place where he can experience a new beginning. Through this prayer we affirm the sacramental nature of the rite while giving it a personal and intimate focus. After that, we should cue the penitent about the way to begin. If we are using a form in which he has the first words to say, it is helpful to suggest, "Why don't we pause for a moment in silence and then, when you feel ready, begin by asking for the blessing?" If using a form where priest and penitent begin by praying together, we could say, "Let us begin now by saying the opening psalm verses together" or "When you feel ready, begin to say the psalm verses and I will join in." What we want to avoid is an awkward silence, with the penitent unsure whether it is up to him to break it.

During the part of the rite in which the penitent is telling his sins out loud, the priest has to be ready for a fairly long spell of very attentive listening, especially in the case of the first confession of an adult. It is often helpful in these cases, and even when a confession might be relatively brief, to signal to the penitent in gentle and unobtrusive ways that we are in fact listening closely. If we have our eyes closed in order to concentrate, and keep very still during the confession, he might get a disconcerting feeling that we have drifted off or "zoned out." Very gentle interjections, just murmuring "yes" or "hmm" at key junctures, can reassure the penitent that he is being genuinely heard. Experienced confessors often find themselves murmuring these signals not just in a random way, but by a kind of inner prompting that has registered something specially significant in the confession.

While confessing their sins, penitents may experience at some point such strong feelings of pain and shame that they break into weeping or seem unable to continue. This situation calls for words of encouragement such as, "Don't be surprised at feeling grief so strongly. Christ is with you in a very tender way at this moment. He said, 'Blessed are those who mourn.' Just receive that blessing and continue with your confession when you feel ready. There's a box of tissues on the table, if you need one."

Occasionally, someone may finish confessing her sins and, in the emotion of the moment, lose track of the fact that there is a final part of the prayer of confession in the rite, which it is now up to her to complete. If an awkward silence suggests that this is what has happened, the priest simply gives her the cue she needs: "Why don't you offer all this to God now by finishing the prayer of confession, where it says, 'for these and all my other sins. . .'?"

What happens next? We can be sure that many penitents will feel vulnerable and perhaps uneasy that their confession was inadequate. Some may imagine that the priest is judging their confession to be threadbare or poorly prepared. So it is often a good idea to begin responding with a brief word of reassurance: "Now just allow yourself to feel tremendously grateful to God for trusting you with all this knowledge of your own humanness and neediness. You were ready for it, and now God has the opportunity to show you how his love completely enfolds all that you were ashamed of." Or "Let's remember how much joy God feels when we hand over to him all these things that give us pain to admit, and remind ourselves that his love includes all the sins we've forgotten about, too."

Giving counsel in confession is such a rich and many-sided topic that the whole of chapter four is devoted to it. In practice, this means that in the space of a few minutes we have answered any questions that the penitent may have and given some words of support and counsel that help bring home the good news of God's generosity, tenderness, and mercy. And we may invite him to say a particular prayer or read a certain

Scripture passage after the confession as a means of further absorbing the message of forgiveness or as a pointer to amendment of life.

Absolution is normally accompanied by the ritual of laying on of hands. The pastor rests her hands on the head of the penitent, reciting the prayer of absolution by heart. There is no need to apply any pressure or to bend over him. It is usual for the penitent to kneel, but if this is physically impossible or stressful, he can be standing or sitting. Whatever posture is being used, we need to avoid encroaching thoughtlessly on the penitent's personal space at this vulnerable time. Discretion prompts many confessors to stand slightly to one side when laying on hands rather than directly in front.

The laying on of hands is a sacramental gesture used in rituals of healing prayer, and pastors do well to anticipate that some penitents may have an unusual spiritual experience at that moment, which is felt as a flow or a rush of energy. Here is a firsthand account of this occurrence:

> I think I came to confession mainly with a sense of blockage in my relationship with God from a lot of shame and resentment I felt about the terrible relationship I had with my father, who died last year. There was a lot of wrong on both sides, and I just had to own up to my role in making it worse by nursing resentment. When it came to the absolution during my confession, to my amazement the priest's hands on my head seem to become really hot and I felt—how can I describe it?—as if a kind of magnet was pulling my insides into a kind of new alignment. There was a sort of column of energy that seemed to flow through me for a moment. After I got up I felt a huge sense of relief. I just had to ask the priest whether he had noticed anything unusual. He had felt this heat I referred to, and assured me that experiences like this

show that forgiveness and healing grace is penetrating
very deep layers in our hearts."

The final words of the rite, usually a form of dismissal, bring the confession to an end, and the penitent rises to her feet if she has been kneeling. This is a vulnerable moment of transition that calls for sensitivity on the pastor's part. Exchanging the peace in the way that is normal practice at the eucharist may be appropriate if offered with restraint and dignity, but anything like a bear-hug, however well intentioned as a gesture of warmth and acceptance, may be felt as erotically charged at this moment. Taking off the priestly stole indicates that the rite is complete. We may close with a simple invitation to remain or to go into the church to offer prayer of thanksgiving. As normal conversation is resumed, we take care not to say or do anything that may seem overpowering or jarring. The pastor should also refrain from remarks that could sound patronizing or banal, such as, "Well, that wasn't as bad as I bet you thought it was going to be, was it?"

Most penitents will have brought some notes on paper that they used in naming their sins, and they may need a simple reminder that this is the moment to destroy them. If the rite has taken place in an office, the pastor indicates a wastepaper basket so that the list can be ripped up and thrown away there and then. If a confession has taken place in church, the pastor may remind him to tear the notes up before he leaves.

Finally, it is important to resist the temptation to plunge the penitent into conversation about unrelated matters: "By the way, can we take a moment to discuss that problem you were having with filling the rota for coffee hour this summer?" We want him to stay with feelings of gratitude for forgiveness, and to be in the right frame of mind to pray briefly in church along the lines we have suggested in the pastoral dialogue, or when he has returned home. After we have bidden farewell to the penitent, we may offer a prayer of thanksgiving for God's grace and then resume the other work of the day.

CHAPTER FOUR

Giving Counsel, Comfort, and Direction

As we reflect more deeply on what is entailed in hearing confessions, the prospect of offering counsel may trigger considerable uneasiness. Just what is expected of us when the penitent has finished her confession and awaits our response? Will we have something pertinent, helpful, or insightful to say to the one who has just entrusted her confession to us? Are we wise enough or holy enough to speak God's word in this situation? Now it is our turn to feel exposed, perhaps even judged: will she consider us a "good confessor" when we are done? If simply receiving the confession has demanded a certain vulnerability from us as well, we may feel even more painfully "on the spot" when it comes to our own response to what we have been told. Perhaps it is not accidental that at this juncture we share something of the penitent's sense of apprehension. But for grace to be fully released in this most humbling of sacraments, both penitent and confessor have to set aside any desire to save face or to rely upon personal qualifications. While our own habits of spiritual practice serve as an essential preparation for this ministry, still in the moment we must hand ourselves over to God in utter trust.

It is frequently said that we are not required to offer any counsel at all. This is true—the validity of the sacrament does not rest on counsel being given or received. Obviously, it would be foolish to press on in emergency situations when time is short, or when absolution is given *in extremis*. But in most cases, failure to offer a word of comfort or encouragement seems cold, and the absence of any comment could be unsettling for the penitent. Without a human response to what has been confessed, the rite can feel mechanical and something less than an incarnation of grace. Why pass up this clear opportunity to speak of God's way with this person just now? Some pastors think that if a confession seems complete, it requires no further comment from the confessor: better to say nothing than risk issuing platitudes. But a penitent is usually feeling far from confident as to the adequacy of his confession, and can feel highly vulnerable after confessing his sins. If we say nothing at all in response to a confession, but simply move on to conclude the rite, he may be left wondering what we are thinking. Depending on the content of the confession, he may worry that the priest either considers his sins too awful to discuss or, at the other end of the spectrum, that his confession was judged thin, trite, or banal. Even when the rite of reconciliation follows a pastoral conversation or session of spiritual direction—when most of the ground has already been covered—still the intensity of the sacrament seems to call for a few distilled words summing up the grace discerned at that moment. Often, those brief words are far more memorable that the many words exchanged an hour before.

The counsel, comfort, or direction offered in confession covers a wide range of possible responses. What should be the spirit animating our words? By tracing the notions of "counsel" and "comfort" back to their roots in the New Testament, we come to what Scripture calls "paraclesis." "Comforting" does not mean cushioning, mollifying, or soothing, but encouraging, strengthening, reviving, and stimulating to action. In counseling we are actualizing the activity of the Counselor, the Paraclete—the Holy Spirit, who makes Christ present and brings to mind Christ's words as living and powerful realities. In direction, we are pointing to where Christ's invitation and call can be discerned and interpreting how Christ is acting now in a particular life.

It is sometimes difficult for pastors new to the ministry of sacramental reconciliation to appreciate how very different this approach is from the way most of us have been trained in clinical pastoral education or similar venues. Some schools of pastoral counseling impress upon ministers the need to be "non-directive" or "non-judgmental," whereas others focus on problem solving, whether short or long term. None of these models is apt for offering counsel in confession. To be sure, when engaged in this ministry, we often come across people who could benefit from sessions of professional counseling, and we might recommend that they seek these out. But even if we have the requisite expertise, we cannot try to tease out problems or issues at great length. Confession is not the setting for this kind of therapeutic work; we do not have time for it, and besides, our role in administering reconciliation is of quite another sort.

The response we can uniquely offer has the primary characteristic of strengthening proclamation. We are proclaiming to penitents the gospel as it personally and immediately applies to them here and now. We strive to announce how God is gracious to them, and how Christ is with them in their present circumstances. We point to his summons to follow him, and we speak of his invitation to abide in him anew.

Just as it is easy for someone trained in pastoral counseling to slip into a rather horizontal, therapeutic mode that is out of keeping with the rite, other ministers are prone to serve as moral coaches. They seem to think that the counsel offered in confession should aim at showing the penitent how to stop sinning, and so they are eager to recommend techniques for avoiding temptation or overcoming faults. Of course, people should not throw themselves recklessly into situations that have proved hazardous for them in the past. There is a measure of prudence in the old maxim about avoiding the "occasions of sin" and knowing what these are for oneself. Sometimes the confessor will need to issue a warning about patterns of sinning that are dangerous or serious. In such cases we may need to bring to light whether the penitent has resolved to take certain definite actions to reduce the risk of falling again.

So while there is a place for occasionally offering this kind of pastoral admonition, a moment's reflection should alert us to the danger involved in regularly giving advice in confession. For many sins cannot be overcome by either strategies of avoidance or frontal attack. The roots of sin are deeply entrenched in our souls, and they show up as actual sins when we are caught off guard. The more subtle and intractable forms of sin are like viruses that break out when we are weak or tired. Naturally, we need to practice vigilance, and keeping watch over our thoughts, words, and actions can engender humility if nothing else. But offering advice about ways to eliminate or diminish faults will lead to discouragement. It places far too much weight on human will power and is apt to inculcate a false program of self-perfection. It also may hinder someone from seeking absolution in the future out of shame or self-contempt. "The priest must always be the preacher of salvation not of improvement," advises Kenneth Ross.[24] Our capacity for self-improvement is limited; we are all repeat offenders, and people will return to confession with the same list of sins over and over again. We cannot undo our personal and social history or the personality traits that prompt us to sin along certain fairly predictable lines. Our strengths and weaknesses fall along the same trajectories.

God wishes us to be free from the oppression of sin, but God's way of delivering us from this bondage is usually slow, indirect, and mysterious. One of the distinct graces of this sacrament involves experiencing the mercy of God for the same sins confessed repeatedly over a long period of time. What is genuinely surprising is not our pattern of

---

24 Kenneth Ross, *Hearing Confessions* (London: SPCK, 1974), 42.

sinning but divine love. We cannot tell a penitent that if she would only try harder, or engage in such-and-such a practice, her life will become virtually free of sin. But we can encourage her not to lose heart, because God will be faithful to her whatever her difficulties, temptations, or falls. Experiencing this love is far more transformative than well-intentioned but fundamentally moralistic advice. The counsel and absolution offered in confession can mediate this love in a piercingly acute way.

The confessor, then, must avoid falling into the trap of unnecessarily amplifying the penitent's sense of compunction instead of speaking the more deeply converting language of grace and healing. Severe exhortation, stressing the gravity of this or that failing, should very rarely be used. In the Anglican and other reformed traditions, penitents come to confession voluntarily, which means that we can almost always presuppose free and sincere repentance. The standard tone of counsel in confession is drawn from Christ's words, "Come to me all ye that labor and are heavy laden."

Listening

To "hear" a confession entails listening with the deepest receptivity. With one ear we are listening to the penitent, and with the other we are listening to God. As St. John tells the story of Easter evening, the Risen Lord broke through locked doors to offer his frightened and guilty disciples peace—and he says it twice, for emphasis. Peace should suffuse the atmosphere of every confession. We cannot be in a hurry or anxious about our next appointment, so it is important that we set aside plenty of time when we schedule the administration of this rite. We approach hearing a confession as we approach prayer: with a relaxed, yet alert, openness to grace and a holy expectation of being supplied with whatever is required to discharge this sacred ministry. We will need to lay hold of a measure of interior silence. We must try to quiet our own clamoring thoughts that so frequently compete with the voices of others, and with God, for attention. As we begin this ministry, most of us will be painfully aware of our own shortcomings. What we have before us is an opportunity to surrender ourselves wholly into God's merciful hands.

So we listen to the confession with close attention, taking note of whatever impressions, suggestions, images, and passages of Scripture might gently float into our awareness. The Holy Spirit really does use our intuition at these times, and we need to trust our imaginative responses as they are kindled during a confession. This is a very different process from cudgeling our brains to come up with something to say—a self-regarding activity that inevitably draws us away from both the penitent and from God. The Holy Spirit will give us wise and life-giving words if we stay open in faith.

The Holy Spirit will be working through the penitent, too. The Spirit has already brought this person to contrition and has led him to seek the grace of sacramental absolution. We are not merely listening to a rehearsal of sins, but to a Christian who has struggled and repented. We are witnessing his gradual and perhaps strenuous liberation from these sins. In the course of listening to the confession, moreover, the penitent himself will often give us hints about what kind of counsel will be apt. As one experienced confessor writes, "The clue lies in listening to the person rather than to the list of sins. . . . One of the things I have learned is that over and over again the penitent tells you what to say."[25] We listen for what he is revealing about his dilemmas, failures, sin, and grace, and these often unspoken realities are woven into the material of the confession. We might ask ourselves: What would be good news for him? What is he seeking? How is God present to him now? How is the mystery of Christ unfolding in his life?

In our response we do not need to comment on every aspect of the confession, and in most cases it would be a mistake even to try. We may notice that some underlying sin seems to connect otherwise disparate aspects of a confession—greed, for instance, or resentment. Or

---

25 John Gaskell, "Not as Judge but as Pastor," *Confession and Absolution,* 149–50.

we may suspect that one particular sin, like envy, is a key symptom of inner spiritual needs that cry out to be met, and we want to say something about that inner need and how God can fulfill it. It would be a good form of counsel to suggest this interpretation to the penitent and, if she concurs, invite her to ponder how God might be offering to supply what has been missing in her life. Sin is misdirected energy; it is love for the wrong thing, as St. Augustine astutely observed. What stirs us to greed and covetousness? Is there a more profound hunger that has not been acknowledged or met? What triggers resentment? Perhaps, at base, a loss of hope, a failure to be grasped by the vision of faith that in the end God's justice will be accomplished and "all will be well." If the penitent resists our suggestion, we might explore what she herself thinks about her underlying motivation, and not press our initial hunch.

On some occasions we may want to focus on a specific element in a confession, especially if the penitent indicates that certain matters are highly troublesome. If we are unsure how to proceed, we can always ask a question like: "Would it be helpful to look more closely at X and Y, and think about what God is inviting you to do?" If nothing draws our attention, we can merely ask, "Is there anything in particular you would like counsel about?" For some people, confession is the only setting in which they feel they can safely discuss their soul's health and their all-important relationship to God. Most penitents will be grateful for our concern and guidance.

There are some whom we will come to know quite well spiritually because we serve as their regular confessor. In hearing their confessions, we will seldom be surprised, yet we can note and give thanks for the steady changes grace works in them over time in ways they may not notice themselves. In the case of these penitents, in particular, the axis of temptation/gifts will tend to be more apparent. We will observe more clearly how their temptations and sins fall directly along the same frontier as their strengths and gifts. As we learn the art of giving counsel in confession, moreover, we may find that the most valuable and enlightening direction we offer will not focus on the sins that have been confessed, but the gifts that the pattern of sinning reveals. For instance, someone who regularly garners attention and laughter by mocking others clearly has a considerable gift with language. If someone knows how to manipulate others, or how to gall and irritate them, then he has innate psychological acumen. So rather than use a rhetoric of blame about "curbing the tongue," we can speak of his misuse of precious gifts. Since God needs people to be articulate and sensitive, just how is God inviting him to use his natural endowments for the sake of the kingdom? Such counsel will often come as a grace-filled surprise. Without in any way minimizing the gravity of the sin, we can redirect attention to God's gracious purposes. Repentance can become the occasion of laying hold of gifts that St. Paul would assert are for "the common good." Instead of harping on the sinfulness of verbal cruelty, we can point to God as the giver of gifts and the privilege of being called to use them in the service of Christ and in personal union with him.

In many cases our counsel will conclude with a recommendation that penitents seek some grace of divine reassurance, a strengthening of faith, or a widening of their horizons to be able to glimpse something of their situation as God sees it. This counsel would contain both elements of paraclesis, or comfort: it proclaims that they are loved and cherished by God just as they are. But it does not stop there. It goes on to ask where the invitation from God may be found in this moment. Christ's words to blind Bartimaeus are our guide here, for Jesus did not presume to know what this man wanted, but rather asked him, "What do you want me to do for you?" For all of us, healing involves putting our desires into words, and saying what we hope to receive from God rather than assuming that God already knows. Sometimes, then, confessors will need to encourage penitents to articulate their desire for inner healing of a spiritual disorder—sins that have led to all sorts of damaging, faithless behavior in the past. Such counsel looks for the remedy not in willpower but in responding to Christ's invitation to ask, seek, and knock. Instead of urging someone to exert tighter control, we instead encourage her to focus on her sense of spiritual poverty, using it as a springboard to imagine the good she lacks and then boldly seek it as a gift from God.

The classic form of counsel, then, comprises brief words of gospel proclamation that speak of God's gift of forgiveness, the invitation to hand over every burden to Christ, and the prospect of a fresh beginning. We encourage penitents to seek what they really need from God. We might do this after a few questions have clarified the situation, or we might use our own words as they occur to us spontaneously. But the core of our counsel might well consist in telling a story from Scripture or reading a biblical passage that speaks to the penitent's condition. The confessor who has a Bible at hand may be moved to introduce briefly, and then read, a passage that contains a message of encouragement and renewal of life. For example, if you have just heard the confession of a pastor who labors under a sense of frailty and inadequacy, you might be led to read part of 2 Corinthians 4, where Paul speaks movingly about how ministers of the gospel are themselves fragile, earthen vessels. Or you could read from the end of John's gospel where the Risen Lord rehabilitates Peter after his threefold denial by inquiring into his love and renewing his commission as pastor to his flock.

The same passage from Corinthians could also be used to assure any penitent that Christ's living presence in us can coexist with feelings of affliction, confusion, and weakness. Even more, the suffering and fallibility most people experience in themselves can be seen as opening them up towards compassion. Without glamorizing pain, we can assure them that God can use every experience of struggle and infirmity, emotional turmoil, depression, and even lapses into sin, to create in us a sense of solidarity with other human beings. Without minimizing the damage caused by sin or the pain of inner distress, and without indulging in cheap reassurances, we can still lead someone to see how God embraces her whole self, including her weakest and darkest side, and can use her for good.

Asking Questions

Frequently confessions will contain material that is too general or too hazy to give a clear picture of the sin actually committed. For someone to admit, for instance, that he has been "proud" or "impure" or "behaved inappropriately" really amounts to nothing more than acknowledging that he is part of the human race. As confessors, we can pass over these sorts of verbal smokescreens in silence, realizing that both God and he know what is behind the vague language being used. But this kind of avoidance on the part of the penitent and confessor seems to undermine a fundamental purpose of private confession: to name one's particular sins openly and candidly. It may be that the penitent is unaware that pride, for instance, is a "capital" or "root" sin that can manifest itself in any number of ways and lead to many other kinds of sin. For example, pride can cause us to refrain from apologizing when we have wronged someone else. It can prompt us to chronic overwork or the neglect of our health and personal relationships in our zeal to achieve success, or make us so turned in upon ourselves that we fail to notice another's suffering. Pride can get us to spend far too much money on items that pander to our personal vanity. The variations are almost endless.

Asking a question or two to move a penitent towards greater specificity in confession shows that we have been listening carefully to him and taking him seriously. It also gives him a chance to open up, to say more about what has been burdening him. It can give him the opportunity to recognize and name what his sins really are. Above all, it helps us minister to him. For instance, we could say, "You mentioned pride as one of your sins. Can you give me some idea how pride shows up in your life? . . . Ah, so you are catching yourself becoming competitive with your colleagues, is that it? Not sharing information in a spirit of teamwork?" It may be that this particular person needs to articulate just how he has been undermining community through personal ambition.

Confessing to anger can often be a red herring, since not all expres-
sions of anger are sinful. Sometimes anger is justifiable, as when we
are responding to an injustice done to ourselves or inflicted upon
another. The desert tradition asserts that God gave us anger to fight
the demons. So some kinds of anger can be useful! What is not per-
mitted is destructive violence of any sort, retaliation, or a desire to
humiliate or hurt. So a confession that acknowledges "anger" without
embellishment usually needs further exploration. Even acknowledging
anger towards a friend, colleague, or family member might mean anything from passing irritation to physical abuse. We could begin, "You
say you have lost your temper with your children. What happens when
you become angry? What do you do?" This distressed parent needs to
be more specific and "open her grief."

The chapter on preparing people for confession suggested that
they try to grasp the root sin that may lie behind specific sinful acts.
Sometimes we will come across someone who confesses only the outward behavior with no suggestion of inner motive. In these cases, we
cannot attempt to delve into what might lie behind everything that has
been confessed. However, we could select one sin to discuss that might
help the penitent gain a measure of self-awareness. Simply asking,
"Why did you gossip about her?" may elicit the reply, "Because she is
always putting everybody else down." It is better to indicate that sins
have many sources, some of which are sinful in themselves: "People can
gossip for all sorts of reasons—because everybody else is, and we want
to feel part of the crowd. Or we might do it out of spite—to get back
at someone who has hurt us. Or out of envy, and so on. Do you have
a sense of what prompted you to gossip in the case you've mentioned?"
Of course, underneath the causes we can easily identify, there may
lurk still deeper layers of unconscious need: feelings of inadequacy, for
example, or misgivings about one's worth. It may be that the confession
will reveal these psychic wounds, and in that case our counsel might
urge prayer for healing or assurance.

Our counsel, however, should remain simple. Even sophisticated people benefit from a clear message or straightforward recommendation. Those who feel overwhelmed by the intricacies of their character or confused by a convoluted situation need simplicity above all. When we do encounter a genuinely complex issue calling for prolonged and involved help, we can invite the penitent to see us on another occasion or to seek another competent person for confidential pastoral or therapeutic care.

Questions need to be put in a restrained and respectful tone. We should never use language that belittles the penitent, and we should never assume the worst. When asking a question, our way of phrasing it should be as neutral as possible. We do not want her to feel defensive, insulted, or so boxed in that it becomes even harder to admit that the sin was graver than first appears. So we ask something like, "What do you do when you're angry?" and not "Did you hit them?" It is entirely contrary to the generous spirit of the sacrament to be tactless or rude, embarrassing the penitent and provoking needless shame. Since we are there to represent Christ and his church, her dignity, privacy, and freedom to say what she wishes to say must be honored. Our questions should never pry into irrelevancies, and it is especially important to exercise reserve when dealing with sexual sin. Because sexual lapses are usually a very tender area for penitents, and because any whiff of voyeurism could jeopardize the integrity of the rite, we must be careful to conduct our discussion with the right mixture of tact and forthrightness.

It can be beneficial, then, to help focus the confession by a bit of sensitive questioning about the sins that have been confessed. However, the confessor should not go looking for other veins of guilt that may have been overlooked or omitted in the penitent's confession. Karl Rahner, in his extensive work on the history and practice of this sacrament, insists that questions must never be posed to uncover an unconfessed guilt. We deal only with the material penitents bring to their confessions, whatever else we may know or think we know about their lapses in other areas.

Restitution

All our sins damage the fabric of our common life and weaken the body of Christ. Sacramental confession of even the most secret and private sins enacts restoration to the community of faith, since the confessor represents the church. As a liturgy of the church, the rite of reconciliation is communal by its very nature. The inner life of the church is also strengthened by the practice of confession, as one member of the body is forgiven, healed, and renewed in the baptismal life. This social dimension of both sin and grace stretches forward, too, as the penitent considers how sin might be avoided in the future and how damage for past sins might be repaired, insofar as restitution is possible. In some cases, penitents will need to exercise their best judgment about what can or cannot be done to set matters aright. Sometimes the one we have injured is dead and thus beyond our present reach except through prayer, or has disappeared from our lives and we cannot track him down. Sometimes recalling the memory of a past injury will do more harm than good.

But in many cases we can indeed do something concrete toward mending broken relationships. We can apologize in person, by telephone, or by letter. If we have damaged someone's reputation by gossip, slander, or detraction, we might be in a position to take back our words or at least balance them with a more positive assessment on a future occasion. We may need to offer to pay for hospital bills or therapy for someone we have injured physically or psychologically through our neglect, lust, or malice. If we have stolen property, we must return it, and if we have secured professional advancement by falsifying our credentials, we must acknowledge our lie. We cannot continue to benefit from something we have taken illicitly and still repent of our misdeed. This is the dilemma faced by Hamlet's uncle, who still enjoys the throne and wife for which he has murdered his brother. Unwilling to forfeit his gains, he at least has the honesty to realize that he cannot pretend to repent.

A penitent may need counsel on whether to acknowledge certain

sins to those whom he has injured, if the injured party is unaware of
the sin. Here are some points that might bear on our counsel. The penitent must ask himself whether he is motivated by a desire simply to get
something off his chest or whether he believes that such a confession
will actually benefit the relationship. A friend does not have to know
that you have spoken ill of her, nor does a spouse have to know about a
secret adultery that is over and done. In some cases it is the better part
of charity to bear these burdens ourselves, after unburdening them to
God and the church through confession, rather than afflicting another
with knowledge of our sin. In making this decision, moreover, we must
consider both our intentions in pursuing a more public disclosure and
the likely result of doing so. Depending on the relationship and prob-
able response, we may also need to tell. A marriage, for instance, may
be so damaged by a clandestine affair that the couple will need professional help to restore it, or a partner may have been put at a health risk
without knowing it, and in that case the truth must come out.

We may also have to guide penitents through the moral calculus of
weighing the likely benefits and possible liabilities of openly acknowledging a crime. If someone has embezzled money from her company,
for example, it must be returned. Does she have to report her theft
to her boss, and thereby lose her job, with slim likelihood of being
employed elsewhere? What if her family depends on her for their live-
lihood? If the stolen money cannot be restored without disclosure, she
must take that risk. But if she can set things to right without public
acknowledgment, she may be justified in keeping her misdeed secret
so long as no one else stands the risk of being blamed if the books do
not tally up as they should. By the same logic, no one has to turn himself in to the police for a crime so long as no one else is in danger of
falling under suspicion. In the early church, certain capital crimes were
excused from public penance for this reason. However, if someone else
might be in jeopardy because the penitent is free and presumed innocent, then he must take steps to ensure the safety of others. We have

already discussed the case of child abuse or other situations where the innocent or vulnerable populations could be in danger. The protection of the innocent outweighs all other considerations, and in these cases true repentance demands that the penitent take all necessary steps. In cases of addictive or compulsively injurious behavior, a sincere desire for "amendment of life" generally requires him to secure competent professional help.

When someone confesses a sin for which restitution might be expected, therefore, we should be listening for some indication that amends of some sort are being made. If she has not expressed any plan or course of action, we might ask about this at the conclusion of the confession. It may be that the penitent has already done everything that could be done and simply did not think it necessary to say so. As we raise these questions, we will want to be careful to allow the penitent to take the initiative in proposing appropriate restitution or amendment. Only in very rare cases should we insist upon a particular course of action. Wise pastoral care seeks to develop Christian responsibility along with an informed conscience. We would want to help her think matters through by exploring the options available to her rather than by telling her what to do. Once again, we will be best served by open-ended questions such as, "Is there any way you can offset this damage to your colleague's reputation?" or "After this long estrangement, is it possible to reach out to your sister? How do you think she might respond to that?" Restitution or amendment may well require difficult actions or changes in behavior, but they are integral to the grace of reconciliation and emerge from it as fruits of true contrition.

Acts of Thanksgiving, Prayer, and Penance

For a long time it has been customary for the priest to suggest some action to be taken or some prayer to be said after the confession as a token of repentance. This is a vestige of the arduous penances that were required prior to absolution in the patristic church and in some of the medieval penitentials. These strenuous and often prolonged acts of penitence were intended to offset a penitent's former sinfulness by a form of ascetical re-education, thus setting the seal on his contrition. It sometimes seems that in earlier centuries of the church, coming up with an appropriate penance, of making "the punishment fit the crime," was the principal work of the confessor. While it is true that acts of personal self-discipline or "mortification" such as fasting can serve for spiritual training, these practices, valuable in themselves, should be separate from the rite of reconciliation. If not, they can obscure the gift of grace freely offered to penitent sinners through Christ and lead to the theologically erroneous notion of earning forgiveness. Acts of restitution or amendment, by contrast, are not penances but rather necessary consequences of contrition.

Likewise, as we have seen, the priest may well suggest certain topics for prayer in the course of giving counsel in confession. For instance, we may propose that a penitent seek a particular grace from God or spend time in prayer for someone with whom she has confessed having difficulties. This approach can be extended as an "act of thanksgiving" that reinforces the message of the counsel. A particular prayer arising out of the counsel of confession offers an occasion for deepening its grace. Typically the priest suggests a passage of Scripture or a psalm for reading or meditation that would amplify the grace experienced in confession. The prayer should not be burdensome or complicated and—like acts of restitution—the confessor should discuss it with the penitent.

Another benefit of recommending acts of thanksgiving lies in their power to move someone past the stage of grief or remorse into gratitude and praise for his liberation from sin. Thus it gives him a way of affirming and experiencing anew the release of forgiveness, redirecting him into a place of worship and joy, and giving permission to leave his regrets behind. Acts of thanksgiving should be performed only once, however, and the priest should make it plain to the inexperienced that this is to be done privately, shortly after the confession or later the same day. It is entirely appropriate, then, for the confessor to suggest that the penitent engage in some form or prayer or short meditation after the confession. This practice is not a penance, but an expression of renewed joy in Christ.

PART TWO: EXAMPLES OF CONFESSION AND COUNSEL

"The clue lies in listening to the person rather than to the list of sins. . . . One of the things I have learned is that over and over again the penitent tells you what to say."

—*John Gaskell*

THIS SECTION OFFERS a series of sample confessions, each one accompanied by the confessor's response. In most cases, the penitent will have concluded the confession with the words of contrition found in the rite, which are not reproduced here. All these situations are, of course, entirely fictional, composed to suggest various types of confession a pastor may expect to hear and to illustrate many of the guidelines for giving direction and counsel set out in the preceding chapters. Sometimes this counsel will take the shape of a pastoral dialogue between priest and penitent.

A first confession by a middle-aged professional woman

The main thing I need to confess is letting God drop out of my life when I was in my mid-twenties. I stopped going to church, and just let prayer kind of fade away. I didn't have crisis of faith or anything; I just became preoccupied with my career. Between that and juggling the demands of my family, there didn't seem to be any time for God. So I lost interest in God, and now that my faith has come back to me after twenty years, I feel ashamed of having turned my back on my relationship with God. It's become really central in my life again ever since I went on a retreat with a friend without exactly knowing why I agreed to go with her, but I had a very deep experience of God's love when I was there.

Looking back now over my whole life, I want to confess all the other things I feel sorry for. I recognize in my life as a child a smug pride in being the favorite, the good child, and I used to make my younger brother take the blame for things I had done wrong. I remember taking money from my babysitter's purse and lying about it when challenged.

In my teenage years, I cheated on several tests, and basked in the kudos of getting high grades based on my deceit. I used several relationships with boys to satisfy my curiosity about sex when I had no intention of taking them seriously as potential long-term boyfriends. I used to ridicule and demean my father behind his back and took my mother's devotion completely for granted without ever expressing much gratitude.

In my years as a college and graduate student, I confess that I was so competitive that I took pleasure in the difficulties and setbacks that some of my friends experienced. I started to find excuses for skipping the eucharist on Sundays, and let people at the chaplaincy down by being half-hearted and unreliable in the responsibility I had taken on there.

In my family life, I confess to resentment against my mother-in-law because I never felt she accepted me. I was cold and cutting towards her, and gave my husband a hard time about their close relationship. She died a few years ago, and I feel guilty now that I never worked things out with her, even though I began to feel more sympathy towards her as her health broke down. I took the line of least resistance when it came to my husband's agnosticism and gradually let the issue of faith just go away from family life. I look back and see that I let my children down over this. I confess that I didn't stand up for principles I believed in when our friends made racist remarks in our home.

I also confess to becoming so caught up in my career that I didn't pay attention to the kind of person I was turning into. I became very committed to our own high standard of living, but I didn't give much thought to the real purpose of my life or to making any kind of contribution to the community.

Now that I am back in the life of the church, I confess I haven't fully joined in the life of our little community. I guess I'm staying on the edge a bit because I still feel a bit unworthy, given my history. I am coming to confession because I know I need God's help to put my years of avoidance behind me, so they don't hold me back.

Counsel

Think of the joy God must be experiencing just now. He touched your heart during your retreat with a sense of his love. Continue to be grateful for that breakthrough. And now your coming to confession is a wonderful sign that you really have returned to God and the life of the church. Remember what Jesus said about there being more joy in heaven over one sinner who repents than over the ninety-nine who didn't need to? So think of how God is welcoming you with joy.

In your confession you spoke of "letting God drop out of your life." Well, of course it must have seemed like that. But in fact God always remains with us lovingly even though we may stop being aware of this closeness. God always has been near you, looking for the opportunity to bring you back into the experience of his love. Jesus told the parable of the shepherd who leaves his flock to go in search of one sheep that got lost so that we will remember at times like this that he has been constantly reaching out to find us again.

Now that prayer is full of meaning for you again, remember it can bring healing to aspects of our life that seem too late to change. You mentioned feeling regret that your mother-in-law died before you had established a better relationship with her. Remember you can pray for her now, and you can ask God to give her your love. God is able to connect you in a loving way so you can be at peace.

You are sad that you didn't raise your children in the faith. Gently entrust their spiritual future to God's care. In his own good time God will find a way to touch their lives. In the meantime, the fact that you are taking your faith seriously now might open new questions for them. Just be yourself and trust in God's grace. St Paul teaches us in one of his letters that the whole family of someone who believes is holy, even though the other members don't yet have faith. Remember God is enfolding them in his arms already.

In a few moments you will be receiving absolution, the assurance of God's forgiveness. Accept it gladly as the sign of a new chapter in your life. There is no need to keep going over the past—now you can think of who you can become thanks to God's grace. There's no need to rush at being active in your church community. But after this new milestone in your life, you can simply ask God, "What part would you like me to play now in my faith community? Show me how I can be of service." You don't have to figure it out right away, but do remember that God sees you as a person who has gifts to offer, and trust him to show you how to use them.

I mentioned the Parable of the Lost Sheep, and sometime today I would like you to find a Bible and look it up in chapter 15 of Luke's gospel. Read the parable again and simply express your gratitude that Jesus has found you.

A teenage girl on a youth retreat

What I want to confess and what has been bothering me for a long time is that I've been having sex with my boyfriend since last summer. I knew we really shouldn't be doing it, but I kind of ignored that. But this retreat and the talks with the other kids here made me have to face what we've been doing. It's not really Christian, is it? I mean, sex before marriage. We've talked about breaking it off, but then we just do it again. But this time I know we have to stop.

I've been telling a lot of lies to cover it up with my parents. They're very trusting so they believe whatever I tell them about where I'm going or what I've been doing. I've lied to my teachers, too, about where I've been after school, say, when I miss soccer practice so we can get together. Come to think of it, I've also copied other kids' homework sometimes and handed it in like it was my own. And then I let other kids copy from me, especially in classes I'm good at.

I guess I should also confess that at the parties I've been going to there's a lot of drinking going on and I've been part of that, too. One time I got really sick afterwards. Of course, that's meant more lies and sneaking the stuff in and hiding it.

Another thing that came up in the talks is how we treat each other. There's this one girl at school who everybody makes fun of because she's fat and wears stupid clothes and tries to fit in, but the more she tries the more everybody mocks her. I don't really dislike her, though. She's not mean or anything, and I know her dad's been in the hospital a lot. They say he has cancer, and that must be awful for her. But I don't stand up for her or even talk to her. She usually eats lunch by herself. I think I'll try sitting with her sometimes and ask about her dad.

Counsel

Now is a good time to remember how much God loves you and takes a deep interest in how you are growing and developing. God is on your side as you struggle with this need you're really aware of—the need to be honest and truthful. Being in a place where you have to tell a whole of lies isn't good. God must be glad that you listened closely to some of the talks that have been offered this weekend. You let them connect with these issues you are struggling with. You may remember that Jesus said to his disciples that "the truth will make you free," so let's think about the kind of freedom you can explore now.

First, be honest with your boyfriend about your need to break the pattern you have been in and change to being close and affectionate without having sex. You aren't pushing him away, but you need to change to a way of relating that won't involve all that deceit you had to use. Talk with him about how you want to be together. Then be honest with God. Ask God for help and guidance and share what you feel. God is on your side. And be honest with yourself about your own need to have boundaries that work for you, that help you keep a sense of the integrity and sacredness of your own body. This is all part of growing up to be ready for sex in the context of a loving, lifelong relationship, which we know is what God wants for us, and offers a way to be truly happy.

In your confession you mention this opportunity to show some initiative in being kind to a girl who isn't very popular or considered attractive. Taking this opportunity to be kind is another way of being honest, too. You can be honest about your own desire to be a generous person who is prepared to ignore what the group thinks in order to reach out in a thoughtful and caring way to someone who needs companionship. God must be glad that you want to let this caring side of yourself show.

Sometime today, spend a few moments thanking God for the gift of forgiveness and this fresh beginning in your life and tell him that you are grateful for the changes that are taking place within you. Christians speak of these changes as signs of the Holy Spirit at work in our lives.

A businessman in his forties who has made a lunchtime appointment to make his confession to a priest he does not know

Thank you for seeing me when I'm not a member of your parish. I just felt that my own rector is too much of a personal friend to be the right person for this. Here's the thing—I had a shocking dream a few weeks ago that jolted my memory about something embarrassing that I seemed to have successfully covered over since it occurred. What makes this really complicated is that I am just about to start my term of office as treasurer in my parish, and what I have to confess makes me nervous about going forward with this step.

About six years ago, when I was still living in Vancouver, I helped organize a big fund-raising event for a local hospice, a kind of street fair. Well, it involved far more work than I had bargained for—it was frantic, but a success. I kept $300 in cash that I could get away with not accounting for. I told myself that it was compensation for all my extra efforts, and my own finances were tight at the time. Now I feel very ashamed. I don't know whether I should tell my priest and offer to withdraw from my appointment as treasurer. Do I need to tell my wife? I don't know how to make it right. I have never thought of myself as a thief.

Counsel

Priest: Let's begin with gratitude to God. We can be sure God wants to use the re-emergence of this painful memory to do something very good: to help you put this theft behind you, make amends, and experience the relief of forgiveness and a fresh start. May I ask you a question to clarify something? This seems to have shaken your confidence in taking up a position of trust handling money in your own church. Besides this sin you committed six years ago, has there been anything else that is making you feel untrustworthy for this responsibility?

Penitent: Well, no. I do tend to worry about my own personal finances and just how much I can afford to give to the church and so on. But this is the only time I've ever stolen money, except—well, when I was a boy I used to take loose change from my grandmother's purse from time to time.

Priest: Remember that God is always ready to forgive us and create a fresh start. There's a simple way you can repair the hidden damage you did by withholding the money that belonged to the hospice. Are you willing to make a donation for that same amount, or even more, to the hospice in Canada?

Penitent: Yes, I can do that. Do I need to give a reason to anyone?

Priest: If you and your wife share all these kinds of decisions about money, and she expects to know exactly why you are making this gift, you will need to give the real reason rather than lie. But exposing your sin to the hospice authorities or to your own parish priest won't necessarily do any good, and might possibly do harm.

Penitent: That's a relief.

Priest: Here's my counsel. Jesus encouraged us to "ask, seek, and knock," and your confession highlights several things for you to pray for. First, ask God for the gift of trustworthiness and ask him to bless your ministry as treasurer of the parish. Second, Jesus did warn us about being anxious for our own security because it deters us from being generous. Maybe that's what led you astray. So ask God for a spirit of trust that you will have your own needs met, and ask God for the gift of generosity.

As a sign that you have taken God's loving forgiveness to heart, would you be willing to pray Psalm 103 right after the confession or sometime later today? This is the psalm that has these strong words of reassurance: "As far as the east is from the west, so far has he removed our sins from us. As a father cares for his children, so does the Lord care for those who fear him."

Penitent: Psalm 103? Yes, I can do that, I've got some time to go into the church now before I'm due back at the office.

A woman retreat leader and spiritual director

I accuse myself in particular of hypocrisy, doubt, and lack of faith in God. I haven't given up my practice of centering prayer, but I feel bored with it and restless. I don't seem to have any attraction to God at all, and when I am at the eucharist I can't seem to keep feelings of disappointment with God and with myself at bay. I seem to have lost interest in religion!—and yet I still give some spiritual teachings in my prayer group, and I see my regular people for spiritual direction. After a session in which I seem to have found a way to guide others, I sometimes say to myself, "What a fake you are!" I am not panicking yet, but these feelings of hollowness make me dread that I might be losing my faith. In fact, sometimes during my centering prayer, one kind of distraction I suffer from is wrestling with thoughts—they are almost like mocking voices—such as, "Who do you think you are fooling? Aren't you wasting your time? Does God even exist?" I hardly recognize myself now, remembering the deep spiritual experiences I have had over the last ten years.

Counsel

This may sound strange to you, but as you were making your confession the phrase "I believe in the communion of saints" came into my mind. I think it might be because at times when we feel shaky and precarious in our spiritual lives, we need to rely on the support and counsel we can get from women and men of God who have gone through what we are going through. All the saints who have followed the path of deep prayer tell us that sooner or later it will take us through some pretty rough terrain. Perhaps we have relied on feelings of warmth and conscious devotion to sustain our sense of intimacy with God. We tend to forget that there's a virtual consensus among the mystics that a time is bound to come when God, as it were, allows our consciousness of his presence to be eclipsed. Then we might have to act almost blindly, and learn a kind of radical dependence on God's grace without being able to find anything within our own feelings to give us much of a foothold.

You are in a genuine time of testing, and the force that St. Ignatius calls "the enemy of our human nature" would be gratified if you began to mistrust the genuineness of your gifts and your calling, or if you began to be preoccupied with self-accusation. Here are some of the recommendations that our friends the saints might offer us during the kind of inner weather you are experiencing, when fog seems to have set in.

Gently remind yourself that you aren't in control of feelings of devotion, and you're not in charge of the inner weather of your soul, either. Let go. Tell God that you want to rely on his hidden grace to endure a period of dryness. God is at work in you just as much when things are dry and dark as in times of light and solace, and the fruitfulness of the spiritual direction you offer is quiet evidence of this grace. Your centering prayer is actually working when it helps bring to the surface the doubts and anxieties you've been experiencing. Don't be afraid of them. When they arrive, calmly greet them and bless them with the name of Jesus.

Our repentance is simply turning to God again, isn't it, and letting go of preoccupation with ourselves? For your penance, will you spend a short time of meditation, gently pondering these words from chapter three of the letter to the Colossians, "You have died, and your life is hidden with Christ in God"?

A gay man in his mid-thirties preparing for a commitment ceremony

Before we begin, let me tell you the main reason for my coming for confession. My partner and I have been going to a counselor to help us prepare for our civil union and commitment ceremony. We have been together for five years and we want to take this step and then go on to adopt a child. This is a big threshold for me to cross, and I realized a confession could be a help in giving me a sense of a new beginning. I have only made a confession once before, and that was my way of taking the fifth step in my program as a recovering alcoholic ten years ago.

I confess that I kept on pushing back against my partner's desire to be formally committed because I was reluctant to pledge exclusive sexual fidelity, and that has caused him pain and confusion. I haven't been promiscuous exactly, but I have flirted and played around sexually on occasion, with an old friend, and there have been a few "chance encounters" when traveling for work. But I do want to make that pledge of exclusivity now. I confess that in a previous relationship I did bully my partner sometimes, and used to attack and humiliate him over his ineptitude about finances. I guessed I liked to think of myself as the strong one who had to be more responsible in the relationship.

I confess that I have held on to resentments against my father, who was angry about my coming out. He was okay with my sexuality only if I kept silent about it. I suppose I have been punishing him by staying out of touch except for phone calls on his birthday and at Christmas. Now that my mother has died and he is alone, that seems mean and childish. I realize it's time to reach out to him again.

I confess to attitudes of scorn and contempt towards conservative colleagues at my office, and I lash out with ridicule about their political positions. I sometimes do the same with other Christians who condemn homosexuality. I also confess that I haven't been good at expressing gratitude, either to my partner or to God. Our AA program recommends the practice of gratitude as an important part of recovery, and I realize I tend to avoid making my gratitude list or giving thanks, even though I know intellectually how healthy it is to practice.

Counsel

I am glad you mentioned gratitude as a key, and I want you to think of the sacrament of reconciliation as an expression of gratitude in itself. We give thanks that God has chosen us, that he won't let us go, that he works with our flaws and failings and is full of hope about our continued growth.

You are about to make a covenant of faithfulness, and that is a sign that you are growing up in Christ and learning from him. Repentance is a kind of willingness to grow up, isn't it? Think, then, of Christ as your inner ally as you grow into your own manhood. He is really more on your side than you are yet! So this is a time for you to trust that he is at work in your relationship, and that he is preparing you for the responsibility of fatherhood. Soon your child will be a new center for your life, a new outlet for your ability to love and care. As a committed partner and a father, you will be stretched and you will learn and you will grow. And you will discover new depths in yourself.

As a response to the absolution that I will pronounce in God's name, I am going to suggest that you set some time aside today to go over in God's presence the good gifts of your life, your work, your partnership, your home, the gifts of recovery and your program, the prospects of fatherhood, and opportunities for reconciliation with family members, especially your own father. And when you give thanks, remember to include the gift of forgiveness that he gives so unhesitatingly and generously.

A rector in his late thirties who comes regularly to his spiritual director for confession

I need to confess how very angry I've been about the behavior of two vestry members. They've been stirring up trouble in the parish because a vote didn't go their way—you know, making phone calls to people whom they suspect would sympathize with them and basically undermining our process. I know that on one level I'm justified in being angry over this, but I've become obsessed with it and just can't get it out of my mind.

I've tried talking to these two men, and they sort of admit they violated our norms for handling disagreements, but then quickly justify themselves by saying that it's just too big an issue to be decided by the vestry alone. I've tried taking the matter into prayer, but that only seems to make my anger worse. I keep going over why they're wrong and I'm right.

There are some other things I want to include in this confession, too. Two months ago I missed my daughter's ballet recital because I had scheduled a meeting at the same time. I should have rescheduled the meeting because she was really disappointed that I missed her event. She had a special role and was really proud that she had been selected for it. I told her that I was sorry that I wasn't there, but I feel a cloud hanging over us. I simply don't know how to make it up to her.

And I have to admit that even when I'm home, I am often preoccupied with work. I'm not writing sermons on family time, but I'm thinking about the parish or making plans in my head when I should be paying attention to my wife or children. I think of myself as a good listener when people come to see me in my office. Why can't I be more of a pastor to my family and really listen when they talk to me?

And then there's my prayer life—still something of a struggle. I do manage to read Morning Prayer most days, but that time for quiet prayer that we've talked about so often seems to elude me. Instead I start thinking about all I need to do and feel so agitated that I just can't seem to settle down. But sometimes—it usually hits me during the eucharist—I just long for something more, for being closer to Christ.

I forgot to take my turn this month offering the eucharist at the nursing home. When the recreation director called me about it, I covered over my lapse with a lie about a parish emergency. I find it hard to go to the nursing home, and I can't help but think that's why it slipped my mind.

Counsel

You're right that your anger is at least partly justifiable. God is grieved, as you are, when people act in damaging ways, and in this case you are concerned, as well you might be, about the unity of the parish. So you will have to continue to deal in pastorally responsible ways with the trouble that's been set in motion. But your confession shows that you're beginning to notice that there's something more going on here; their sin or selfishness has somehow got its hooks in you. It's not only disturbing your prayer, as you observe, but the lack of inner freedom that you're experiencing will also make you a less effective pastor. Just what the Evil One would want, isn't it?

So you might consider what this situation is revealing about your own points of vulnerability and weakness. We really can't control the behavior of other people, can we? And that helplessness of ours, especially when we feel responsible for others, as you do for the parish, is hard to accept. But it's a place where we can grow into Christ's own weakness—his utter refusal to control others—and discover the strength of divine love. Accepting our helplessness in cases like this doesn't mean giving up on these men, nor does it mean that you should stop trying to set matters aright. But it does mean giving up the illusion of control that we like to harbor when we feel hard pressed. By accepting everyone's freedom in this situation, including the terrible freedom to sin, God can renew your own deepest freedom to minister to others with a sense of peace. Venting your anger in prayer was an honest and humble way to begin; maybe now it's time to acknowledge your sadness, vulnerability, and weakness. Make it an act of oblation, offering these painful feelings to God, and then wait in the darkness of faith to see how God will act.

Maybe owning up to this sense of weakness can help with your family, too. Listening requires receptivity on our part—a readiness to receive something. If you don't know how to get past this impasse with your daughter, why don't you ask her for help? Family life can teach us how to forgive and be forgiven. Children learn from us that we can mess up badly and still move forward, provided we're humble enough to admit we were wrong. Why don't you ask her how you can make it up to her, whether you can make it up to her, and see how she responds? And I will continue to hold you, the parish, and your family in my prayers.

A single woman in her fifties making her confession to her parish priest during Lent

I've missed saying my prayers sometimes. I didn't go to work twice, called in to say that I was sick, but I was lying. I'm impatient with my mother. When I go out with my friends I sometimes drink too much. I've gossiped, maybe three or four times. I waste time on the Internet and watching TV. I could have helped out with the children's pageant—you know, they asked me to—but I said I was too busy. That was a lie, too.

Counsel

Priest: It's good that you've made your confession now during Lent. You have confessed to several different sins. May I ask which one bothers you most?

Penitent: Well, I guess impatience with my mother.

Priest: And why is that?

Penitent: Because she can't help it that her mind is starting to go. She asks me something, and the next day she asks me again. I hate to see her like this! It gets on my nerves. But I know I've got to be more patient. I've been asking God to make me more patient.

Priest: Were you close to your mother before this?

Penitent: Oh yes, I used to be able to talk with her about anything, and we'd do fun things together.

Priest: And now it seems like she's slipping away?

Penitent: Yes, and I have to admit I don't like the person she's becoming. She never asks anything about me anymore. I know that sounds selfish and maybe it is.

Priest: I think you're trying to be honest about your struggle to be kind to someone who used to be there for you. It's hard not to feel angry and sad when someone we love—and who has loved us—starts to disappear from our lives, or dies. But you also say that you were blessed with a closeness to your mother for most of your life.

As an act of thanksgiving, spend about ten minutes today recalling some of the things about your mother for which you feel most grateful, and give thanks to God. Don't be surprised if sadness comes mixed in with these prayers. It's part of what Jesus meant when he said, "Blessed are those who mourn." Your mother hasn't died yet, but she is slowly dying to you.

And now with absolution, receive with faith the grace of dying to all the sins you have confessed and the grace of rising to new life in Christ—the mystery we will soon celebrate at Easter.

A man in his early forties, the owner of a small local business, married with three young children

I want to confess that I'm not the father or husband that I should be. Family life isn't at all what I expected. Everything seems chaotic from the time we get up until the kids go to bed. I really lose my patience with the kids a lot. Almost every day there's some kind of scene, and some-times I blame my wife for it when it's not really her fault. I guess I'm just worn out. We both are, really. I haven't hit the kids, not ever, but I've felt close to it. Still, I yell at them more than I should, and when I do, the

two-year-old sometimes gets frightened and cries and that makes everything worse.

Sometimes I drink too much, especially on weekends, just to relax.
I've also been masturbating because my wife is usually too tired for
sex. I think a lot about a woman who works in my office. I love my
wife, I really do, it's just that things are hard for us now. I find myself
wondering what happened to the spark between us, and sometimes I
resent the children for all the energy they take just to keep up. But I
know that's stupid, too, because I love these kids. I just wish I could be
a better dad: more patient and less stressed out by the noise and mess
and, you know, just ordinary kid misbehavior. I've prayed that God
would help me be a better father but I'm still failing.

I think I also need to confess the way I envy my brother—or maybe
more, my brother's money. We're doing okay financially, but my brother
was always the star of the family and he's gone on to make loads of money.
When they came over for Christmas, they gave us really expensive gifts,
stuff we wouldn't buy for ourselves, and of course we couldn't reciprocate.
At first, I felt he was putting me down, but when I thought about it a few
days later, I realized that they were just trying to be generous.

Actually, I have a lot to be grateful for: a good wife, three healthy
kids, a decent income, even my brother and his wife, and this community. What I'm hoping for in this confession is that God will help me be
the kind of husband and father I know he wants me to be.

Counsel

Your desire to be the kind of husband and father God wants you to be
is a grace in itself. Wanting to be more loving and patient is actually the
work of the Holy Spirit in you. The uncomfortable part of the Spirit's
work—which you're also feeling and which your confession shows—
makes you aware of your shortcomings and failures in this regard.

I want to encourage you to continue to pray for the patience,
strength, and wisdom that the vocation to marriage and parenting
requires. Family life, for those who are called to it, is a place of deep,

ongoing conversion. It's where God gets really close, and God some-times shows up as our crying children, having our plans upended, or living with noise and mess. It takes so much love—more love than we have ready at hand—to live this vocation. The sense you have that you're not up to it sometimes doesn't show that you're hopeless, but rather that you're honest. When we can admit that we need God's grace for very ordinary things, maybe just to get through the day, we're close to the condition the gospels call "poverty of spirit." Don't be afraid of feeling that you've run out of your own resources. It's humbling, of course, but it can be a springboard for real prayer.

In the meanwhile, I suggest that you also try to tend your relation-ship with your wife. When was the last time you two went out together to do something you both enjoy? You can barely remember? Could you begin to think about how you can make that happen once in a while?

Finally, it was grace that helped you come around to seeing the envy at work in your initial response to your brother's gifts at Christmas. Envy has a way of poisoning our relationships and draining them of joy. You ended your confession by naming some of the things for which you're grateful. Thankfulness is the opposite of envy. Envy takes us into the realm of fantasy thinking: imagining that we'd be happier if we had someone else's good fortune, or resenting others for what they have or seem to have. But a sense of thanksgiving—the thanksgiving God has already stirred within you—keeps us grounded in the truth that all our blessings are sheer gift. As an act of thanksgiving for the grace of abso-lution, would you pray Psalm 32 sometime later today?

A mother in her late forties requesting a discussion with her parish priest before they begin the rite of reconciliation

Thank you for hearing my confession last month during the Lenten Quiet Day. It really means a lot to me that we have you, a woman, as our new rector. I feel I can unburden myself more easily to you. But I bet you weren't expecting to see me again so soon—we haven't even got to Palm Sunday yet! I've got a problem, though. You know that part of the rite where you asked me, "Do you forgive those who have sinned against you?" I said yes, because what you had to say about forgiveness in your second talk had really moved me. But a couple of days later day I started feeling I had lied. There's someone I don't forgive. I feel I just can't. You know all about the scandal we had here in the parish seven years ago, so you can guess who I am talking about. My son Dan has had such a hard time as an adolescent coping with the experience of having been sexually abused by that priest who used to be on the staff here. I have felt such hatred—hatred!—for what he did to my lovely kid and some of his friends. It took a lot of counseling to help me with the terrible sense of failure I had for not recognizing the signs that something bad was happening. I just told myself I had a moody kid! I know that pedophile was drummed out of the priesthood, and now I've just heard from a friend on the west coast that he died of a very aggressive cancer around Christmas. I feel I can never forgive him, and now that he's dead I can't work through it. So my last confession wasn't really sincere!

Counsel

Priest: I'm glad you are bringing this up and haven't struggled with these feelings alone. You have found yourself in a place where Christ can be a healer for you. Your rage as a mother is something Christ empathizes with. He didn't hold back when he expressed the intensity of God's pain over any harming of children. In fact he spoke with devastating frankness about it—better for someone to have a millstone hung round his neck and be thrown in to the sea than incur the guilt of hurting one of God's children!

Now the possibility of forgiving this man for his crime would have come up if, during his lifetime, he had truly taken to heart the enormity of his sin and had come to you and your son, in grief and deep repentance, to ask for the gift of your forgiveness. Forgiveness is a gift, not a right. Then you would have faced the challenge of finding it in yourself, with Christ's help, of reaching out to him in mercy to help lift his burden of guilt. But strictly speaking we can't forgive anyone who is not seeking that gift of mercy from us. It is a person-to-person exchange.

Well, now he has died that can't happen, not in this life. So we move into different territory. A way forward is possible. The power to forgive comes from our Christian experience that we can share "the mind of Christ." We can resonate with Christ's love for others. We can let Christ's attitude towards them influence our own feelings and behavior. And we believe that the man who injured your son, and hurt you so badly, is in Christ's presence now and is having to experience the full awareness of his sinfulness and his need for mercy and healing. Even if he is out of direct reach, do you think you might be able to find it in yourself to want him to be transformed and healed and forgiven by God's love?

Penitent: Now there's a challenge! But if you put it that way . . . I know I don't want anyone to be damned. Do I want him to be healed? When we had counseling, it was explained to me that virtually all sexual abusers were themselves victims of sexual abuse. I guess I want God to win in the end! So where do I go from here?

Priest: Don't be upset by recurring feelings of anger towards this man. But whenever you have feelings of resentment towards him, quickly pray like this: "Okay, Jesus, he is all yours! Over to you. May your healing love change and heal him." Jesus did ask us to pray for our enemies, not to pretend that we haven't been their victims. Just pray for him whenever he comes to mind and let him go into the tough love and mercy of God.

Penitent: That's possible, I think. It doesn't make me go into denial. I can try that. So now I don't feel a confession is really called for today. I can come when the need arises in the future.

Priest: Of course. Let's just have a brief time together for prayer now, and I will give you a blessing with the laying on of hands, praying for healing and the help of the Holy Spirit, and asking God to help your son.

A soldier who has recently left the army after three tours of active duty in Iraq and Afghanistan

Father, you don't know me from Adam, so let me just tell you a bit about myself. I have just left the army, and you may have seen me with my parents in church for the last few Sundays. I'll be staying with them while I start looking for a job and then getting a place of my own. I spent the last six months in military hospital—my foot had to be rebuilt after a combat injury. Well, let me get to the point. I feel like hell because I have killed innocent people. I won't attempt to describe what mayhem some of the combat operations out in the villages turned into. But I know I have killed men in their homes. I believe it must have been my bullets that took down a couple of women in the chaos. In my nightmares I cry out, hoping to God that those two kids we found dead after the smoke from grenades had cleared . . . that I wasn't their killer.

I entered the army in good conscience. I am a patriot and I believe our country is trying to do the right thing over there. When I signed up, I knew I'd have to kill soldiers, but it's all the others—the women and children, and the men who weren't involved one way or another—that makes me feel I have blood on my hands. When I was being treated in the hospital, I had some talks with the army chaplain, and he worked hard to ease my conscience. But he couldn't grasp that I really feel guilty, even though I don't know what else I could have done. I don't blame him for not understanding because I can't understand what happened, either. My heart is ripped about those innocent lives I took in the madness of war. I need God's forgiveness, but I don't know how he can forgive me, when I don't know what else I could have done.

The penitent breaks down and sobs. The priest pushes a box of tissues within his reach and waits quietly for several minutes, leaning towards the penitent, but not touching him until the penitent himself reaches out his hand to be grasped.

Counsel

I do remember you coming up to receive communion last Sunday. The choir was singing, "O Lamb of God, you take away the sins of the world, have mercy upon us." You have come in deep, deep need to have your sins taken away, and when it is a matter of taking human life, we need to know that God's love knows no limits. It is deep enough to take away the sins of the whole world, the worst that human beings can do to each other. Whatever your precise guilt is here, God's love is greater than any wrong we can ever commit. Sometimes it takes the most terrible pain that the conscience can feel to open us up to God's compassion and readiness to forgive. Sometimes our guilt is so intertwined with that of others that we can't quite unravel the strands, but that shouldn't keep us from seeking God's mercy and receiving it. The cross of Christ shows itself to be good news only to those who know the depth of our need for its saving grace, as you do. Jesus gave himself on the cross in order to meet you with love just where you are now.

You have undergone a terrible ordeal, and in time you may come to understand it with greater clarity. But God sees the whole of it with perfect truth and infinite compassion. You say your heart has been ripped open—God can use this widened heart of yours to be an instrument of his peace in this violent world. You just don't know how yet. In time, and as you slowly move into civilian life, God will show you.

One of the ways you can express your sorrow and repentance is to pray for those who died in the battles in which you took part. Our freedom to pray for the dead, all of them, is a wonderful gift. Whoever they were, they are now in the hands of a merciful God. Through Christ your sorrow and love can reach them. One day, in a way we can't begin to imagine, we will all be reconciled within God's embrace.

After the confession is over, make your way into church to give thanks for the gift of God's forgiveness. On the back wall you will find a shelf with Bibles. Take one and find the twentieth chapter of John's gospel. In the middle of the chapter there is the scene where Jesus comes into the upper room on the first Easter Day. For the disciples, Good Friday was full of confusion, too, and they felt sad, helpless, and guilty in its aftermath. When Jesus appears to them, he shows them his wounds in his hand and side. That's how they recognize him, and then he offers them peace.

This is how he comes to you now. He shows his wounds to let us know that he suffers with us in the worst we can do to one another. And he brings peace. You can show him the wound in your foot and your heart. He recognizes you, and all that you have gone through, and brings you peace and forgiveness.

A member of a young mother's group in a suburban parish, brought up a Roman Catholic, whose only previous experience of confession was in her teens

I confess to gluttony, and I've also been extravagant, going shopping and buying all sorts of stuff we don't need and can't afford. Plus I feel terrible when my husband makes me take things back to the stores, and when he gets "that look" on his face—I can tell he's worried that I'm on track to becoming obese. I also confess to laziness. It is has been six years since I worked outside the home. Now the twins are settled at school, it is time I was earning again to help us out, but I just can't seem to get going.

Counsel

Priest: You know, there's a reason why there are so many stories in the gospels of Jesus healing people. People were drawn to Jesus because he seemed to understand what it feels like when something has gone seriously wrong in our lives. So coming to confession is a bit like a doctor's appointment with the Lord—and you have brought up in your confession some of the major symptoms, like food. Would you say your eating is out of control? What is that like?

Penitent: When I am on my own I raid the refrigerator—ice cream, bagels, cheese, the whole lot.

Priest: Do you notice how you are feeling when you get the urge to go on shopping sprees?

Penitent: Well, I say to myself, "Shopping therapy time!" It's because I feel I need a boost. If it wasn't for the mother's group, I'd be really lonely. I have a hard time liking myself.

Priest: When we behave in a compulsive way, it's usually a sign that we feel empty inside. Food and shopping can soothe those feelings. But they can't take the ache away for long, and we end up feeling worse about ourselves than ever. The Holy Spirit can use those feelings, painful as they are, to alert us to what's wrong and to bring us to Christ. You have responded to the Spirit's prompting by coming to confession; it is a sign that deep down you know it is time to turn things around.

Can I suggest that you think of this appointment with Christ the Great Physician not as a one-time thing, but as the start of a healing process? To repent really means saying to the Lord, "Count me in, can we work out a plan to get me back to health?" As part of that process, I would like to suggest you make a private appointment with me to talk about a way forward for you. It might be that Overeaters Anonymous could be a great help to you. It has been a godsend to some friends of mine, and there's a group that meets to work that program over at St. Stephen's Church. If we look a bit more into your feelings of sadness and being stuck, we might come up with a way for you to get further help with that through counseling. And I can suggest ways to pray that might help get you back in touch with the tender love and regard God has for you.

Penitent: I didn't feel I was worth taking up anybody's time, but I see what you're getting at. I suppose my gut was telling me that I do have spiritual issues. Now that I don't have the kids all day, perhaps it's time to rebuild my own life a bit. Thanks for your offer of help.

Priest: God loves you deeply, so listen to the prayer of absolution that I am going to pray as Christ's representative. Let the prayer wash over you as a sign of that love and as a pledge of God's desire to bless you and heal you deep inside. After confession, spend a few moments in prayer in church. Right after absolution I am going to give you a Bible to take with you into church and open it to the passage where Jesus healed the blind beggar, Bartimaeus. Read it carefully. Notice how Jesus asks him, "What do you want me do for you?" That's what Jesus is asking you. So tell him about the changes you'd like to make in your life and ask for his grace and strength to make them. (Just leave the Bible on the altar when you are through, and I will pick it up later.)

A confession made in his hospital room by a truck driver who is about to undergo open heart surgery

I'm glad to see you, thanks for coming. You've got communion there, right? Before I receive, there's something I want to get off my chest—something I've never told anyone since I moved here fifteen years ago.

This operation tomorrow has me worried and I know I might not pull through. But even if I do, I want to know that I'm all right with God.

Priest: Are you saying that you'd like to make a confession? That you'd like to use that sacrament to experience God's forgiveness?

Penitent: Yes, I need that. I'm glad they gave me a private room, so only you will hear what I'm going to say.

The priest opens the prayer book to the Rite of Reconciliation of a Penitent and briefly explains the flow of the prayers.

Eighteen years ago—I remember it to the day—I was involved in a terrible accident, and it was all my fault. I'd been driving a truck for two years by then, and I realized I could bring in a fair amount of cash by taking on long hauls. I was young then, cocky, I guess. I used to press on driving even when I was dog tired. One day it caught up with me, and I fell asleep at the wheel, going a good 60 mph on the highway. Next thing I knew I woke up in the hospital with some fractured ribs and a broken arm and lots of bruises. And then they told me that my truck hit a car straight on. It was a family—parents, three kids. Killed them all. They didn't have a chance, not against my huge rig.

There was an investigation, of course. I was acquitted. Couldn't help it if I fell asleep, right? But I knew I'd been taking a chance, driving too long, being greedy. Wiped out a whole family! Of course I prayed God for forgiveness, over and over. And maybe God has forgiven me. But I'll never forgive myself. How can I? All those lives cut short! I don't deserve peace, do I? And I wonder if God really does forgive me. If I die tomorrow on the operating table, how will I face him? How will I ever face God for what I've done?

Counsel

Do you remember Jesus' words from the cross, "Father, forgive them, for they know not what they do"? When he was dying in terrible agony, Jesus forgave those who planned and carried out his death. If our Lord could forgive those who were responsible for his death, even giving them an excuse ("they know not what they do"), he will also forgive us when our sins hurt his beloved children—even when they kill them. You know you did not commit murder, which is the intentional killing of another human being. But as you have confessed, you took a reckless chance out of greed and pride, and it had devastating consequences. Even if there had never been an accident, that sin would still be what it was—no more and no less.

There's no getting around the harm we can do, even unintentionally. But the power of divine love is greater than our sins and the wreckage they cause. God raised Jesus from the dead, and the family that died those eighteen years ago are with him now.

"Forgiving ourselves" doesn't mean making excuses for ourselves or letting ourselves off the hook. Repentance means taking responsibility for our sins, just as you have done, and turning to God in sorrow and faith. This confession is part of that turning, isn't it? Reaching out to God for his mercy because we know we can't set things right ourselves? When God raised up Jesus from the dead, something new began for the whole universe. Never before had death been defeated and transformed into life. Something new began for that family when they died, just as something new begins for you with the gift of forgiveness that comes with absolution. "Forgiving yourself" means letting God have his way with you, accepting his forgiveness, taking it to heart, and letting go. Will you do that? Yes? Then after absolution, we'll continue with anointing, so God may continue to heal your broken spirit and grant you safe passage, if possible, through your surgery. And finally, we'll share in the joy and blessing of Holy Communion.